The Unwanted Undead Adventurer  [eleventh 11]  Yu Okano / Illustrator: Jaian

An old giant.

eleventh

# 11 The Unwanted Undead Adventurer

**Yu Okano**

**Illustrator: Jaian**

# Nive Maris

A Gold-Class adventurer and vampire hunter. The closest adventurer to reaching Platinum-class.

# Gharb Faina

Rentt's great-aunt, a medicine woman, and a mage.

# Capitan

Chief hunter in the village of Hathara. Expert spirit user.

# Wilfried Rucker

A Mithril-class adventurer who wields a giant sword. Helped Rentt when he was young.

# Jinlin

Rentt's childhood friend who dreamed of becoming an adventurer. Killed by a wolf.

# Myullias Raiza

A saint in the Church of Lobelia blessed by the spirits. Can manipulate divinity, and specializes in healing and purification

## Summary

Rentt, an adventurer stuck in Bronze-class, turned undead after he was eaten by a dragon. He eventually evolved into a ghoul and, with Rina's help, sought shelter with Lorraine in the city of Maalt. After forming a temporary party with the Silver-class adventurer Augurey in the royal capital, Rentt and Lorraine undertake several guild requests. The trio make smooth progress completing them after gaining the cooperation of the village girl Ferrici, but then a mysterious, cloaked old man appears before them...

# Characters

## Sheila Ibarss

A guild receptionist. Privy to Rentt's secret.

## Lorraine Vivie

A scholar and a Silver-class adventurer. Assists Rentt in his undead endeavors.

## Rentt Faina

An adventurer striving to reach Mithril-class. Turned Undead after falling prey to a dragon in a dungeon.

## Edel

A monster called a puchi suri who lived under the orphanage. Became Rentt's familiar after drinking his blood.

## Alize

A girl living in the orphanage. Dreams of becoming an adventurer. Apprenticing under Rentt and Lorraine.

## Rina Rupaage

A novice adventurer who helped Rentt and dragged him to town after he became a ghoul. Now Rentt's vampiric servant.

## Wolf Hermann

The Maalt guildmaster. Recruited Rentt to his guild.

## Isaac Hart

Serves the Latuule family. Powerful enough to conquer the Tarasque Swamp.

## Laura Latuule

The head of the Latuule family. She collects magic items as a hobby. She requested that Rentt periodically deliver dragon blood blossoms to her.

THE UNWANTED UNDEAD ADVENTURER: VOLUME 11
By Yu Okano

Translated by Jason Li
Edited by Suzanne Seals
English Print Cover by Mitach

Copyright © 2022 Yu Okano
Illustrations by Jaian
Cover Illustration by Jaian

First published in Japan in 2022 by OVERLAP Inc., Tokyo.
Publication rights for this English edition arranged through OVERLAP Inc., Tokyo.

Find more books like this one at https://j-novel.club!

Managing Director: Samuel Pinansky
Light Novel Line Manager: Kristine Johnson
Managing Translator: Kristi Iwashiro
Managing Editor: Regan Durand
QA Manager: Hannah N. Carter
Marketing Manager: Stephanie Hii
Project Manager: Annie LaHue

ISBN: 978-1-7183-5750-1
Printed in Korea
First Printing: April 2024
10 9 8 7 6 5 4 3 2 1

# [ C O N T E N T S ]

# Chapter 1:    Surprise Attack

"Our last objective is a luteum golem," Lorraine said, a wry expression on her face. "Do you think you can manage it?"

In front of her—which meant in front of us too—was a group of the very luteum golems she was talking about. Yep, *golems*, plural. And not just a few of them either. Several dozen of them were gloopily meandering about. Our misfortune was evident: we'd run into the type that was high in moisture content. Incidentally, the spot they were meandering around was at the bottom of a depression somewhat akin to a basin, though I couldn't make a guess as to why they were doing so.

Since they had no escape path available, if we'd been here to hunt them and nothing else, we could've just had Lorraine clean them all up with one of her magic spells. However, our objective was to gather their materials. The mud or clay of a luteum golem was rich in mana and prized as an alchemical ingredient, but as it was also very malleable, one careless brush with magic could render it useless. In short, we couldn't count on Lorraine's help for this; we'd have to use spirit to attack them. Therefore, the job fell to Augurey and me.

"Doesn't seem like it'll be *too* much trouble, so long as we resign ourselves to getting caked in mud," I said.

Augurey shook his head. "No, it won't be that easy. If you let your guard down, you'll find yourself suffocating to dea—" His face lit up in realization, so much so that I could practically read his mind. *But you don't have to breathe, do you, Rentt? How convenient!*

And he was right; this body of mine came in exceedingly handy in times like this. My encounter with the tarasque was one such example. Augurey, on the other hand, not being an undead, reaped no such benefits. While I didn't really mind taking on this fight alone, it would draw Ferrici's suspicion if Augurey didn't go too. We needed to act naturally with her around.

"I can handle this alone if you don't want to get your clothes dirty, Augurey," I said. "You can just stand by in case I need backup."

I tried to pass it off with a haphazard excuse, and Augurey nodded. "I appreciate it, but I'd feel bad making you do all the work. Just this once, I'll make an exception to my personal policy and change my outfit."

He took off his outer garments and stuffed them into his magic bag, then took out a set of plain clothes and put them on. I was touched by his concern for me, but Ferrici's faith in him had probably influenced his decision. Augurey was likely thinking that it might bother her if he just sat back and left all the fighting to me. He was a tactful guy when it came to those kinds of subtleties.

With that, we were ready.

"Okay, here goes," I said, taking the vanguard and sliding down the rim of the basin.

Augurey followed me down. "Try your best not to get us dirty if you can," he muttered to me. "I *do* like these clothes, plain as they are."

When I was midway down the side of the basin, I felt the luteum golems at the bottom focus their attention on us. Their bodies were made of sludge, and I could make out the hollow depressions that served as their eyes and mouths. I still had many doubts about whether those dark eyes could actually see, but currently, they were unmistakably pointed in our direction.

The luteum golems began to advance toward us, oozing across the ground as they did so. By the time we reached the bottom, we were already surrounded and greatly outnumbered.

"They're a lot gloopier up close," Augurey said. He looked depressed.

"I *did* tell you to let me handle this alone," I replied.

"I figured that I'd lose Ferrici's trust if I let you do that."

"I guessed as much. Well, if it looks like you're about to get dirty... Actually, scratch that. If it looks like they're about to try to suffocate you, use me as a shield. Not like I need to breathe, after all."

Although luteum golems attacked in a similar fashion to slimes, they were scarier to deal with. Compared to a slime—a regular slime, at least—they had more brute strength. Additionally, while a slime's main form of ranged attack was its Acid Blitz, a luteum golem had...

"Those are totally aimed at us, aren't they?" Augurey pointed at the swarm of earthen arrows that had just formed in midair, summoned by the luteum golems.

The arrows were instances of Gê Bélos, a human spell. However, that didn't matter to luteum golems, who could use many different kinds of earth magic. For that reason, a basin like this was the perfect place for them; they could attack and defend as they wished. No wonder there were so many of them here.

"Where else would they be aiming?" I said. "First things first, let's cut their numbers down. You know what to do, right?"

"Of course. Smash their cores, just like they're slimes. It'll take some practice to get right, though. Unlike slimes, these golems' bodies aren't see-through."

"You got it. All right, let's do this!"

"Yeah!"

We took off, weaving our way through the crowd of luteum golems, stabbing and slashing at their buried cores as we went.

If I had to praise their species for something, it would be for the fact that they weren't very fast. They weren't exactly *slow*, of course, but their movements were well within our abilities to handle. Nevertheless, that wasn't to say we could afford to let our guards down.

As I continued to fight, one of the luteum golems split its body wide open and headed straight for me, clearly intending to engulf me whole. Usually, this would be a dangerous situation—if it caught somebody, it would suffocate them to death—but that didn't matter to me. I leaped straight into the luteum golem and easily located its now-exposed core. After I smashed it to pieces, the monster melted into a regular pile of mud.

Although this method made hunting golems easy, it would be too dangerous for a regular adventurer. If they messed up, they'd die. It was a good thing I was already dead. The usual procedure of stabbing a golem from the outside was tedious, since even if you vaguely knew where the core was, you'd still need to stab several times to score a direct hit. Thankfully, I could ignore that and make use of the best method for me: diving straight in.

Unfortunately, since Augurey couldn't do—or really didn't want to do—the same, he retreated far back every time a golem opened itself up, whereupon I would jump in from the side and smash its core. It made me feel like I was using Augurey as a decoy, but I figured, hey, whatever works. Besides, this way was just more efficient.

The number of luteum golems dwindled rapidly, and in what felt like no time at all...

"Only one more to go," I said.

"Looks like it." Nodding, Augurey stepped up behind the final golem and stabbed his sword into it, finishing the fight.

After watching it melt down, we looked at each other, each taking in the other's appearance. What we saw wasn't pretty—we were both utterly caked in mud.

"The sooner I get this stuff off me, the better," I said.

"While I'd love to take a bath," Augurey began, "it might be best if we go for a dip in the lake. I don't think the inn would appreciate us getting mud everywhere. Speaking of which, let's not forget why we came here."

The basin was now littered with piles of mud, which we still needed to collect. Lorraine and Ferrici were going to work with us, hence the former's wry expression earlier. She hadn't had to fight, but she still needed to get dirty. Surprisingly, Ferrici seemed to be taking it well; she looked cheerful as she descended into the basin, holding on to Lorraine for support.

"Playing around in the mud like this really takes me back," she said, taking a container from Lorraine and happily filling it with mud. "It's like I'm a kid again!"

That was definitely one way to see it.

And so the three of us, taking Ferrici's pluckiness as an example, diligently set about scooping mud into containers, all the while convincing ourselves that we were having fun.

"And with that, we've taken care of all the requests," I said. I was currently washing myself off in the lake. "That took less time than I expected."

Augurey, who was in the lake with me, nodded. "You're right. I thought it'd take us two or three days at least, so I'm glad we finished up sooner. We pretty much owe it all to Ferrici, though."

The girl in question wasn't with us, and neither was Lorraine. They were washing themselves off somewhere else. It wasn't as if they could bathe with us, after all. I figured that if I went and tried to sneak a peek—not that I had any intention of doing so—I'd get a friendly introduction to one of Lorraine's lightning spells. Seeing as how I was drenched in water, that would probably mark the end of my days in this world. If Lorraine were by herself, she might not have particularly cared about her modesty, but currently, Ferrici was with her. Whatever the case, though, I wasn't going.

"Still, I'm not sure whether to call us lucky or unlucky," I said. I was thinking about all the fuss that had occurred back at the village. If none of it had happened, we would never have gotten Ferrici's help. It was the perfect example of a happy accident.

"You're right," Augurey replied, studying my body as he spoke. "And that goes doubly true for you. Aside from being so pale, you look like any regular human. I kind of want to know what you looked like when you were a skeleton."

Right now, with the exception of our underpants, both Augurey and I were naked, which gave him a full view of my body. However, unlike when I was a skeleton and a ghoul, I didn't have to worry about someone seeing me anymore. Sure, I was a little pale, but that was it.

I also still had my mask on since, as usual, it wouldn't come off. I was shifting its shape around to clean out the mud that had gotten underneath it, and at the moment, it was only covering the lower half of my face. I had the feeling that this was the style I'd been using the most recently. It came in handy when going in and out of towns because guards were less suspicious and more willing to let me pass if they could see my eyes.

"Being a skeleton *really* sucked," I said. "All I could do was rattle around. Being a ghoul wasn't much better, but I at least figured out a way to talk, in a sense. It kind of felt like I was getting a new lease on life."

"If you can call being a ghoul 'living,' I guess," Augurey replied. "Although, I'm not so sure I can say that anymore. Maybe having a human consciousness is enough to qualify it as being a life. You know, because of you, I've been thinking recently about whether it might be possible to talk with any ghouls I meet, among other monsters."

"I think about that too from time to time, but it's probably a no go."

I'd never been able to properly communicate with any of the ghouls I'd met. I wasn't sure why; I'd had a fairly developed consciousness at that stage. What was the difference between me and them? Was it because I was originally a person? Or was it because a dragon gobbled me up? I had no idea. In the first place, what *were* monsters, really?

Lorraine was continuing with her research and conducting all kinds of investigations, and I was doing my best in my own way to squeeze something out of my dim-witted brain, but we still hadn't found an answer for my situation. It was probably no surprise, considering that we were basically looking for an explanation for the existence of monsters, and people had been posing that question since forever.

Lorraine was a genius, but history had many geniuses, and none had ever managed to shed much light on the truth behind monsters—whose origins especially remained a mystery. There were many theories regarding that, but none of them could say anything for certain. I supposed our only option was to keep searching and thinking.

"High-ranked monsters can talk, though," Augurey said. "Vampires and ancient dragons specifically come to mind.

But maybe with ghouls, their communication's closer to something like humans and monkeys. It's a real mystery, isn't it?"

I had no answer for him. I hoped that I would, one day...but I didn't know if that day would ever come.

"Sorry," Augurey said. Maybe he'd seen that he'd thrown me off a little. "Didn't mean to make you brood over it. I was just making small talk."

He was right that I'd been brooding somewhat, but it wasn't as though it had made me depressed or disillusioned with life or anything. I'd just been pondering what it meant to be alive.

"Don't worry about it," I said. "I think about this stuff all the time anyway. You just had me reconsidering what a mystery it all is."

"Yeah? That's good then. Well, it's about time we should be going. Did I get all the mud off?"

Augurey spun around, giving me a clear view of his body. It was slender but well proportioned—the very figure of an adventurer. He looked clean to me, so after asking him to check my cleanliness, we dressed ourselves and headed for the meeting point we'd decided on with Lorraine.

"Looks like we're all clean," Lorraine said upon meeting up. Maybe it was because we'd all been caked in mud only a short while ago, but she almost looked like a new person. "The innkeeper shouldn't have any complaints now. Shall we?"

Our return trip was very comfortable. The difference from our journey here was especially notable when we passed through the mime wyvern breeding grounds, since now we were far less worried about them attacking us. We couldn't completely let our guards down, but neither did we have to stay on tenterhooks all the time. We really owed Ferrici a lot.

Unfortunately, while it would have been lovely to simply finish our carefree trip back, sometimes life just throws lemons at you. We were only a straight shot away from the village when we caught sight of something strange.

"Is that…a person?" Ferrici asked.

The rest of us had already noticed long before she'd asked her question. My eyes could see pretty far, and Lorraine and Augurey knew that something was up from the silent glances I'd been sending their way. The three of us had subtly changed our route as a result, but it didn't take long for the figure in the distance to adjust for that and cut us off.

Whoever they were, they were clearly suspicious. That being said, we had to go past them if we wanted to reach the village. Left with no choice, we headed in their direction. Having to keep Ferrici safe meant that if anything happened, we'd be fighting an uphill battle, but sending her off to take another route alone was also a scary prospect. It was safest that we all stayed together.

We continued walking, and before long, the suspicious "person" was right in front of us. There was only one way to go about this, really, and that was to approach them and talk. They were clad in a cloak, out of which protruded a pair of skinny arms that looked to be an old man.

"Excuse me," I said. "Excuse me, sir? Is something wrong? We'd be happy to hear you out if—"

Before I had the chance to finish, something massive and heavy crashed into my stomach.

What just happened? Lorraine couldn't make head or tail of it. That wasn't surprising, of course, because when all was said and done, she was a mage. Though her combat ability was fearsome, the way she fought was fundamentally different from that of other professions, like swordsmen. Her physical ability still far exceeded any average person's, but even so, she hadn't been able to catch exactly what had just happened.

Nevertheless, she *was* capable of making an instantaneous judgment. *This stranger is dangerous.* Whoever this old man was, he had just sent Rentt flying.

The moment Rentt had approached and began talking, some kind of massive object had slammed straight into his stomach, blowing him far away in the blink of an eye in the direction of the forest and causing him to knock down several trees in his flight path. If it had been a regular person instead of Rentt, they would have died. There was no way they could have survived. An adventurer might have stood a chance of coming away with only grievous injuries, but they wouldn't have been able to make their way back any time soon.

Rentt, however, was different. His body wasn't that of an ordinary human, but a monster. His physical ability was incomparable to an average person's, and so was his durability. In addition, he had Division up his sleeve, which helped him recover from serious injuries in a heartbeat.

All of this reassured Lorraine that there was no chance Rentt could've died from a strike of that degree and that he'd be making his way back shortly. Maintaining her composure, she pulled Ferrici in close and cast the strongest instantaneous shield spells she could manage around herself, Ferrici, and Augurey. She knew that their first priority was to make some distance, so she readied herself to do just that—

"You're slow."

By the time Lorraine's senses caught up, the old man was already right in front of her, his cloak fluttering around him. He had closed the gap in an instant. The old man raised his arm, clearly intending to do something with it—something that was obviously connected to the strike that had sent Rentt flying. Even with danger backing her into a corner, Lorraine didn't miss it, and she knew the next strike would be coming at her, Ferrici, and Augurey. Pointing her wand out, she chanted a spell.

"Ard Harba!"

Even among other earth magic spells, Ard Harba was notable for the sheer amount of mass it summoned. It created a gigantic, sharpened, spear-like shard of rock and sent it flying at the opponent. As spells went, it was exceedingly simple, but that was precisely why it was so hard to defend against. While water, fire, and other such spells could usually be neutralized with their opposing element, throwing a wind spell at Ard Harba would do nothing to get rid of it.

That said, methods to counter it still existed. The reason Lorraine had chosen Ard Harba was because it provided the best means of escape from their current predicament. Naturally, it wasn't the kind of spell a person could easily fire at will without chanting the full incantation. That is, unless that person was Lorraine. Moreover, she managed to cast it while simultaneously maintaining three shield spells—a truly impressive feat.

The massive earthen spear shot straight toward the old man at an incredible speed—

"Ungh!"

But with a grunt of exertion, he deflected it, blowing it away and sending it crashing into the ground.

Lorraine was shocked. She almost couldn't believe her eyes, but logic prevailed. She knew that the world was a big place; there were all kinds of monstrously strong people out there, any number of whom could probably have done the same thing this old man just had. She couldn't afford to let her surprise get the better of her.

In a heartbeat, she gathered her mana, preparing to fire her next spell, but the old man's legs were faster, and he closed the small distance she'd gone to such lengths to buy in no time at all. But the next moment, Augurey, sword held high, stepped in to bar his way.

"Not on my watch!" he shouted.

"If you want to be first, then be my guest!" The old man grinned and raised his arm, and Lorraine got her first proper look at what exactly had blown Rentt away and deflected her Ard Harba.

As the old man lifted his arm, it expanded to a disproportionately titanic size in a fraction of a second. He swung it at Augurey, who was sent flying bodily away. Against so much mass, there was only so much one could do. That was the cold, hard truth.

Lorraine knew that her hastily cast shield spell on Augurey had fulfilled its purpose and absorbed most of the impact before shattering, but it was obvious that it had been unsuccessful in entirely nullifying the blow. Although she lamented the fact she hadn't had more time, she was fairly certain she'd saved him from dying, which was good enough for now. The problem was, things were only going to get worse.

The old man hesitated for a moment, as if wavering over which of his opponents he would make his next prey, before finally tearing his eyes away from Lorraine and taking off into the forest in the direction he'd sent Augurey flying.

"I s'pose I can leave the mage for later," the old man murmured, and then he was gone.

Lorraine was of two minds over whether to pursue, but she had Ferrici with her. She had to get the girl to safety first; she couldn't put her in danger by taking her along.

She could still sense Augurey's mana, so she could tell that he hadn't been incapacitated at least; he was running through the forest. He'd probably be fine for a while. In the meantime...

"Ferrici."

"Yes? Um, what just—?"

"I don't know, but we'll figure it out later. Here, take this. It's a magic item that can cast a powerful shield spell. I've already charged it with mana. Take this too. As long as you hold on to it, I can find you wherever you go. Hide yourself and wait for me, okay?"

Lorraine didn't want to do this, but against an opponent as dangerous as the old man, she had no choice. She, Rentt, and Augurey had to face him together. Ferrici would only get in the way. She couldn't just do nothing for Ferrici, though, so she fell back on this as her last resort. Neither the Goblin nor the Siren were in the area, so at least she didn't have to worry about them attacking the girl.

Lorraine didn't know whether the old man had allies around, but if he did, that was what the shield spell was for. Moreover, the marker she'd given Ferrici could serve as a targeting point at which to fire long-distance spells. None of this was to say the girl was entirely safe, but even so...

"Got it." Ferrici nodded emphatically. "Don't worry about me. Go!"

To her brave words, Lorraine replied, "Sorry! I owe you!"

And then she was off, running into the forest.

"Can't say I saw that one coming!" Augurey said to the old man before him. There was no deeper meaning behind his remark. Augurey just hadn't expected him to be so strong.

The old man had an unusual amount of pure offensive strength. Augurey had barely managed to get the flat of his sword in the way of the old man's gigantified arm before it struck him, but the weight of the impact itself had been staggering. If it'd been a direct hit, he'd have taken some serious damage.

As it was, even though Augurey had somehow managed to defend himself in time, crashing through the surrounding trees had left his back a mess of scratches and wounds. The body of a regular human was frail. He should have either dodged the strike or reinforced himself with spirit and magic and clashed with it directly.

Augurey thought he'd done the next best thing by wrapping himself in spirit right after taking the blow, but it hadn't been enough to protect him. Evidently, his skills still had a long way to go. But while his training might have proved insufficient, he still had his life—which meant he could still do something about this situation.

"Why, did you think I was of the same caliber as *the other two*?" the old man said.

Augurey paused for a brief moment before replying, "Who are you talking about?"

The old man smiled at his feigned innocence. "From that reaction, it's obvious that their cover's been blown. I'm not sure how you saw through them, but I suppose it doesn't matter. That aside, you don't want to make the mistake of lumping me in with them. *They* haven't quite mastered their own strength yet, you see."

Augurey thought he'd done a pretty good job of playing dumb, but maybe the old man's age had made him wise to that kind of thing; he'd seen through the act in an instant. Still, maybe that wasn't surprising, given the situation. The Goblin aside, the Siren's plan had gone up in smoke, with the woman herself ending up captured. It wasn't difficult to imagine that had led the old man to believe everyone else had been compromised too.

That said, Augurey *had* made the exact mistake the old man had mentioned: he'd expected the third member of Goblin and Siren's group to specialize in tricks and schemes too. He'd been convinced that was just how they operated. But instead of getting that, he'd gotten this old man—a physical combat specialist.

People said to face your problems head-on, but there was such a thing as taking sayings *too* literally.

"Are you sure this whole cloak-and-dagger business is a good fit for you?" Augurey asked. "I think fighting in a colosseum somewhere would suit you more, personally."

In many towns and cities, live combat tournaments were a form of entertainment. Places like those were always looking for strong contenders—especially if they had novel fighting styles. In that sense, the old man would make for a perfect contestant.

The old man grinned broadly. "I had enough of that when I was younger. Made me go looking for a job where I'd get to do something other than beat up opponents all day. Luckily, I found one which came with colleagues and all kinds of different employers."

"Colleagues?"

"You've met them, haven't you? They're... Well, let's not dwell on the details. You've got a strange way of dressing yourself up, but you're a man, yes? Men should be silent and let their fists do the speaking."

"And just let you insult my clothes like that? This is *fashion*, I'll have you know—although the concept might be lost on you, grandpa."

"Heh. Then you'd better not let this grandpa get the better of you, eh, kid? That said, maybe it's because of my age, but I've been growing more senile recently. I might forget to hold back."

"If you could forget who your targets are too, that'd be great."

"Lorraine, Rentt, and Augurey, was it? How odd. My aging memory only picks the strangest things to...remember!"

The old man kicked off the ground, making it judder with a terrifying *bang* and leaving an unnaturally huge footprint in his wake. He had probably gigantified his foot at the moment of impact.

Augurey saw the old man's fist coming straight toward him. He knew what would happen next. The old man would increase its size again before the blow landed. Nevertheless, faced with the imminent threat, Augurey stayed calm, focusing all of his thoughts into a single question: *How am I going to fend this off and make my counterattack?*

"Ugh, damn!"

How far had I been blown away? It felt like my entire body was protesting against me. Upon closer inspection, I realized that broken bones were sticking out of my skin all over the place.

In my condition, any regular human would've died. I, however, barely felt any pain, but that wasn't to say the feeling was entirely nonexistent. Maybe that meant if I was injured badly enough, even this body of mine was capable of dying. Although, considering I was already undead, perhaps "getting obliterated" was the more accurate term. At any rate, I'd hardly be able to put up a good fight in the state I was in.

With a bit of focus, I used Division. It felt strange, as if the outlines of my body were getting fuzzy and I was coming apart at the seams. No matter how many times I did it, it felt unnatural. Still, I'd become a lot more used to it, so the process went a lot more smoothly than my earlier attempts.

Maybe my current location had an influence on that too. For some reason, being in the midst of a forest helped me concentrate a lot better. Did it have something to do with the spirit that had blessed me? I wasn't sure, but all the same, I managed to disperse and reform my body.

Whereas before I had looked like a mangled corpse, I was now back to normal. My skin was pale and smooth, and my bones were all back in place, but the scary thing was that my robe wasn't even dirty. It had probably saved me from even worse injuries.

Despite my fresh appearance, though, I hadn't come away completely unscathed. Just like Nive had once told me, Division only fixed your physical state. Suffer too much damage in a short time, and your very existence would become diluted, eventually causing you to vanish into oblivion. Nonetheless, just as broken bones eventually healed, that damage recovered over time. I had to be careful and avoid too many serious injuries in too short a period, but, well, that was just common sense.

The advantage of this was that I could take some major punishment and keep on fighting as though nothing had happened, but it came with the drawback of not knowing how much I could take before I died for good. All of which was to say that Division was very risky. I'd have to be extremely careful about using it. Maybe it was even a contributing factor to why older vampires like Isaac and Laura had such a detached air of calmness to them. That aside...

"This should do. Now, which way did I…?"

After confirming that I was back in top condition, I took the time to find my bearings. I couldn't locate people by their mana like Lorraine could, but my body gave me access to a few special tricks of my own. I could strain my ears and use my sense of hearing, of course, but I could also find my way via the smell of blood…and it was the latter that I was relying on right now. I could smell Augurey's blood, which worried me. I figured Lorraine was fine, given I couldn't smell hers, but…

"I've gotta go!" I took off in a rush. My brand-new body felt strange, creaking and groaning as I moved, but I figured I'd get used to it soon enough.

*You'd better not die on me, Augurey.*

I ran toward the direction I could smell Augurey's blood coming from, not sparing a thought for anything else. Maybe it was because I was in such a hurry, but it felt like ages before I finally reached him.

I'd been able to tell that some kind of fight was happening from the thunderous impacts I'd heard while running, but the scene that greeted me was one of utter devastation. The surrounding trees had been smashed to pieces by some kind of tremendous force, and the ground was littered with large holes that looked like something massive had stomped them into the earth.

How had—?

*Bang!*

Before I could finish my thought, the deafening sound of another impact resounded. It was so violent it shook the air, sending a strong gust of wind blowing over me.

I looked at where it had come from and saw the old man chasing after Augurey, who had been sent flying away. Augurey's back collided with a tree, but it didn't look like he'd lost his will to fight just yet; he was still maintaining his grip on his sword.

By the looks of things, I'd made it in time. But before I could breathe a sigh of relief, the old man raised his fist. Then, with the sudden, odd sensation of space contorting, his forearm abruptly multiplied in size. Seeing the old man gigantify his arm, I finally realized how he'd blown me away earlier.

Back then, I hadn't understood what'd happened, but if he could make his arm that big, then old man or not, it was no wonder I'd felt such a massive impact crash into me. In any case, it was obvious that even a Silver-class adventurer like Augurey would be crushed if he took a direct hit.

I dashed forward, running toward Augurey as fast as my legs would take me.

"Is that all you've got, kid?"

"Hah… I'm not…done just yet…grandpa."

"I see you've still got a mouth on you, at least. A lot of people lose that when their backs are against the wall. I'll give you credit for spirit. It's been a while since any of my opponents have lasted this long against me too."

"What an honor. Still…this isn't over just yet."

"Really now? Then I look forward to what you have in store for me." The old man smiled, half-serious, half-joking, and lifted his arm, gigantifying it again in the process.

*This is bad*, Augurey thought. He didn't know what to do against the old man's attack. Regular methods of defending or evading seemed futile, but what else could he do? The massive arm loomed before him. Was closing his eyes and accepting his fate the only option left to him?

Before Augurey could finish that thought, however, someone grabbed ahold of him and flung him away from the incoming blow. Shocked, he looked over to see who it had been.

"Sorry I'm late. I was dead, you see."

Hearing his friend's familiar banter, Augurey smiled wryly.

"I'll say. A little later and I'd have joined you on the other side."

I had just barely made it. The most dangerous thing about this old man was that despite how huge he could make his arm, it didn't slow him down at all. He simply moved it as though it were a normal appendage. To top it off, he had the agility of a first-class fighter. It was beyond doubt that he was an absolute monster...which, coming from me, was pretty ironic.

Still, "joined me on the other side," huh? Augurey could be a funny guy sometimes. Him becoming undead too sounded fun in its own way. I could've pulled Rina in as well and formed Rentt's Army. We'd be a force to be reckoned with, capable of even taking on Laura's Army...or not. At best, we'd probably just get turned into her vassal state. Although, now that I was thinking about it, Laura seemed like she'd be great to have as a feudal overlord. She'd probably distribute all kinds of wealth, fame, and military might among her vassals.

"Ho ho, what's this? Aren't you the fellow I sent flying earlier? Rentt, was it? I didn't think you were alive."

The old man approached me, cracking his fingers as he came. The fact that he wasn't rushing to close the distance probably meant that he was wary of me. From what he'd said, it sounded like he'd intended his first attack to be lethal. To be fair, it probably had been. The only reason I looked good as new was that I had the unfair advantage of Division on my side. I'd have been dead without it for sure.

"I hate to be the bearer of bad news," I said, "but as you can see, I'm as lively as ever. Or maybe I'm not. It's complicated. Nonetheless, I'm here, and that's what matters."

The old man looked confused. "I assume you mean you didn't escape unscathed? Well, that's a marvel in its own right. It's rare that anybody can take one of my blows and be in good enough shape to talk about it afterward."

"I'll bet," I replied. "I've never been hit that hard before. I don't suppose you'd be willing to let us in on the trick, would you? You know, as an offering so that I can die in peace."

I wasn't being serious, of course. I just wanted to buy a little more time while Augurey recovered his stamina. Surprisingly though, the old man answered.

"Hmph. Why not? Here, look." He raised his arm, and space contorted again as it expanded to the size of the surrounding trees.

Even though it wasn't new to me anymore, seeing it again was a shock. How in the world did he do that?

"There, simple," the old man said.

"Right…" I responded. "I'm surprised you aren't crushed under your own weight."

"I don't train my body just for show. How about a round of arm wrestling? I'll have you know I've never lost."

I was pretty sure that "training his body" was a massive understatement, but at the very least, it was obvious that the old man was capable of supporting the mass generated by his technique. I didn't know if he used spirit or mana, or if it was just a latent special ability of his, but it was amazing all the same. Since his ability was basically inhuman, I even felt a sort of kinship with the old man.

"I'll pass," I said. "I can't go around telling people I lost to a senior citizen."

"I suppose that's for the best. Now then, has the kid over there recovered yet? I'd like to pick things back up, if you please."

The old man had seen through me—although I'd kind of expected him to. I was pretty sure he hadn't played along out of pity. If I had to guess, he'd been taking stock of me as we talked. That made him the kind of person who didn't underestimate opponents just because he'd beaten them before. One thing was for sure; this wouldn't be easy.

"Augurey. Can you fight?"

"Yeah, thanks to you slipping some of your divinity my way. I'm injured, but I'll make do."

This whole time, I'd been healing Augurey, who'd been hiding behind me, with my divinity. Since my power was nothing impressive, and thanks to my studies in healing magic, I'd been able to keep it subtle.

It didn't look like the old man had noticed. Now, it was two against one. If Augurey and I steeled ourselves, we could probably manage this... Right? Either way, it wasn't like we had much choice.

"Here I come then, kids. I'm hoping this will be fun. Don't let me down."

Then, as if ringing the opening bell to a fight, the old man kicked forward off the ground, sending an earsplitting *bang* reverberating through the surroundings.

"Whoa!"

With the *whoosh* of air being split apart, the old man was suddenly on me. Reading that he was going for a horizontal swing, I just barely managed to duck out of the way. I felt the sheer mass of his gigantic arm swipe above my head.

Immediately afterward, I went to put some much-needed distance between us, but the old man was way more physically capable than you'd expect of someone his age. If I didn't at least get a hit in before I jumped away, he'd just close in on me again.

Therefore, I swung my sword hard. It didn't matter where it connected as long as it did. The old man's arm hadn't shrunk back to normal yet, so that would make matters worse for him if my swing landed.

Or so I thought. Apparently, my crude strategy had been a poor choice. Although my sword scored a direct hit on his body...

*Clang!*

It made a sound similar to metal striking metal and bounced right off.

"You're joking?!" I exclaimed.

"Rentt! Watch out!" Augurey yelled.

Seeing that the recoil from my strike had thrown me off-balance for a moment, the old man came at me with his arm a second time. Augurey, having read the movement, shoved me out of the way, just like I'd done for him earlier.

*Wham!*

The giant arm struck the ground, making a deafening impact and kicking up a cloud of dust. Evidently, it had snapped a few trees along the way too, because wood chips were flying everywhere. It was almost silly how much destructive power it had.

"I'm not done yet!" Even with visibility low thanks to all the dust and wood chips in the air, the old man continued swinging. The swings were haphazard, but given the size of his arm, that likely didn't matter. He'd probably figured it was better than waiting for the air to clear.

That would've been the correct decision to make against a regular person, but my undead body had a few useful tricks of its own. My eyes could see the body heat and physical presence of living things, so I could see the old man's arm with no problem at all—which actually kind of scared me, because it meant that what I was seeing was his real arm. It almost made me wonder how a person as strange as him had come to be, but I was in no position to be thinking that of others.

The old man probably had a whole fantastic tale of his own to tell. If we'd met under different circumstances, we might've been able to have a good, long chat about it. He seemed friendly, after all—he'd been happy to show off his ability to us when I'd asked. But, well, this wasn't the time to think about trivialities. I'd hoped it would help me calm down, but it hadn't worked.

Since I'd figured Augurey couldn't see in this mess, I'd grabbed him and was running us around, but I wasn't sure what to do next. I considered my options.

My swing earlier might've bounced off, but it wasn't like it had been the best I could manage—just an on-the-spot attack that I hadn't been able to put all my power into. I could still pack a lot more spirit or mana into my sword. Mana-spirit fusion or even divinity-mana-spirit fusion were options too. The latter was a double-edged sword, but I thought I could manage the former. Probably. Although, if *those* bounced off the old man too, we were done for. I took a moment to wonder if he was even human.

Nevertheless, it looked like the inhuman old man still had to worry about his stamina, at least, because his attacks were coming less frequently. Seeing that, I dropped Augurey off.

"Rentt! What's the plan?!"

"Let's see... How about—? Whoa!"

*Bam!*

A tree flew by like a spear and embedded itself into the ground nearby. In an unbelievable turn of events, the old man was grabbing them and throwing them at us now. The air had cleared, so both Augurey and I had managed to get out of the way, but we definitely couldn't let this continue. After dodging the next attack, I'd—

"Found you!"

By the time I realized it, a massive arm was coming straight toward me.

*I can't dodge this one!*

I readied my sword, hoping to at least avoid a direct hit, but quickly realized it was futile. Left with no other choice, I used Division. My body lost its shape and became a mass of darkness.

"Hmmm?!" The old man cocked his head. It seemed as though that massive arm of his still had a pretty keen sense of touch, because he appeared confused that his attack had lost its target and only connected with thin air. It looked like we both knew that I would've suffered some serious damage if his swing had landed.

"Where did you—? Ah, never mind!" The old man paused for a moment, as if to search for me, but upon noticing Augurey, switched targets. He swung his arm straight down in a crushing blow, but Augurey was far enough away that he was able to avoid it successfully.

This was my chance. I quickly reformed—a feat I owed to my training—and concentrated mana into my sword. Then, I dashed toward the old man and swung it straight at the back of his neck.

I still had a healthy respect for the elderly, of course, but this was no mere old man—something that he proved right away, before I could even decide whether to feel guilty about my attack. I didn't know if it was because of his experience or simply sheer instinct, but he noticed me coming for him and whipped his arm around in a backward swing. It went without saying that he'd also gigantified it.

The swing wasn't very fast—maybe because it'd been off the cuff—but it was more than enough to protect his neck from me. Consequently, my sword slammed straight into his arm. An intense blast of power compressed the air around the spot where it connected and exploded outward with a massive *bang*.

"Ngh!" Unsurprisingly, the old man flinched, then flapped his arm several times and backed off from us.

It seemed I'd managed to get a good hit in. The old man shrunk his arm back down to its regular size, and I saw that the spot where my attack had landed had ruptured open from within. Blood was gushing from the wound, so it looked like I'd done some real damage.

"Perhaps I underestimated you…" The old man ripped off a section of his own clothes and wrapped it tightly around the wound. He then chanted some kind of spell that stopped the bleeding.

I didn't think he was a mage, but apparently he did have some magic in his arsenal. Having a simple spell to stop bleeding was one thing, but it was pretty scary that he hadn't even batted an eye when using it on such a serious injury.

He didn't look like he was going to run, so he was probably still raring to fight. I took that to mean that he thought he still had a good chance of winning this.

Which was to say, unfortunately, this fight wouldn't be wrapping up any time soon.

"Hmm, what should I show you next?" the old man muttered.

"What do you mea—?"

Before I could finish my question, I was interrupted by a shout from behind me.

"Rentt! Augurey!"

I turned around and saw that it had come from Lorraine. She was running toward us across a field of smashed-up trees and massive holes, her face drawn into a scowl.

"Are you two okay?" she asked once she reached us.

"As you can see," Augurey replied, not turning to look at her. While I'd been turned around, he'd kept a close eye on the old man. It was less that he was quick on the uptake and more that we'd just known each other for so long that we instinctively knew how to work as a team—something that I was grateful for.

"So the mage is here too now," The old man said, spotting Lorraine. "Are you sure that girl will be okay alone? I have colleagues of my own, you know, and I don't mean the one you captured."

He was clearly saying it to throw us off our guard, but we didn't know for sure that he was lying either. Lorraine's reply, however, was cold and goading.

"I don't see the problem. We simply have to deal with you quickly."

I could hear from her voice that she'd been unwilling to leave Ferrici behind. She sounded kind of irritated, which was rare for her. The old man didn't notice, though.

"Heh. I suppose that wouldn't be enough to shake you, would it? You're a lot more than we bargained for. It's no wonder my two colleagues weren't a match for you. If only our information had been more accurate!"

"Your two colleagues?" I repeated. There wasn't much point in playing dumb now, but I figured there was no harm in trying.

The old man wrinkled his nose. "You can drop the act already... But ah, I suppose I'll play along. One of my colleagues is a veteran himself but isn't much to speak of in the ability department. He's realized that the merchant's life suits him more, so this was going to be his last job. As for my other colleague, although she has quite the rare ability, she lacks experience, making her too proud for her own good. I intended on this being a tricky job for her, to take her down a peg and allow her to grow."

I wondered if the old man had completely given up on his cover, but I realized that probably wasn't the case. He had likely just decided there was no point in maintaining it anymore. Besides, his goal was to kill us, and as the saying went, dead men tell no tales. Except me, but I was a special case.

The old man continued. "Sadly, neither of them managed to pull it off. Although, that's no surprise, given that the information that got passed down to us was full of holes."

"Passed down to you?" I asked, cutting him off. I hadn't been able to stop myself—that was how badly I wanted to know who his superiors were. The old man glanced at me but didn't answer.

It seemed that even dead men didn't need to know some things. I didn't blame him; nothing was absolute. He'd probably be in trouble if he spilled all his secrets and then we managed to get away. He was right to be cautious, especially since he didn't know how confident I was in my ability to escape.

I doubted there were many people who could pin me down if I used Division. I couldn't say there were *none*, though, considering folk like Nive existed. Adventuring was a profession full of monsters, and Nive was only at the top of Gold-class. Dealing with Division was probably a piece of cake for Mithril- and Platinum-class adventurers.

If I had to guess, I'd say the old man was good enough to put him somewhere in Gold-class—or maybe even higher. Those weren't the type of people you were supposed to just run into on the road, but, well, here we were.

The old man kept talking. "What got passed down to us was that our targets were two regular Silver-classes and a Bronze-class who wasn't even worth mentioning. But what we got instead was you three. A monster who can take one of my blows and look no worse for wear, a skilled fighter who can make me run in circles for a long time, and a mage who can cast an instant shield spell strong enough to guard against my arms without even chanting it. If I'd known you three were our targets from the beginning, I'd have done a lot more preparing. This really isn't worth what I'm getting paid..."

"Then why not cut your losses and go home?" I asked. I figured it was worth a shot.

The old man smiled. "Perish the thought. Worth it or not, work is work, which is why I'll be killing you, even if I have to push these old bones hard to do it. I'll be out of a job otherwise."

Given his line of work, by "out of a job," he probably meant that his life was on the line. The underworld sure was a rough place. I could feel for him in that regard. Still, it wasn't like we were going to hold back. Not that we could even afford to against someone as strong as him.

"Now then, I think that's enough chitchat. I count all three of my targets in front of me, and I'll have you know that I won't be letting a single one leave here alive."

"Do you really think it'll be that easy?" Lorraine asked.

"No. I'll not underestimate you any longer. I wasn't exactly playing around before, but it's time I get serious. Behold! Hrmmm!!!"

The old man began to tense up all over. I didn't know what he was going to do, but I knew that it was bad news.

The three of us weren't nice enough to just wait for whatever was coming, of course. Augurey and I brandished our swords and dashed toward the old man, while Lorraine held out her wand and started molding her mana. However…

"Too slow!"

An enormous wave of pressure shot out from the old man's body, sending Augurey and me flying and creating an intense burst of wind that broke Lorraine's concentration.

"What in the…?"

The violent storm centered around the old man had blown us quite a distance away. When I looked back over at him, I realized that there was now a massive *something* standing in his place.

It didn't take me completely off guard; given the old man's ability, I'd considered it to be a real possibility. But because he'd stuck to increasing the size of his limbs, a part of me had thought that was his limit.

Right now, I was being proven very wrong.

"Is that…?"

"No way…"

In contrast to the mumbles from Augurey and me, Lorraine's words were plain and clear. "He's a giant. I never expected to meet one in a place like this."

Yep. We were looking at an honest-to-goodness giant.

Giants. Although their race had thrived once, long ago, they were hard to come by these days. Compared to the modern age, a much larger, more diverse assortment of races had existed in older eras.

The proof of this lay in the many relics and abundant folklore that still survived to this day. Many of those races themselves, however, were no longer anywhere to be seen. The reason for this was unfortunately unclear, and it was a confounding question for many, because a significant number of the long-gone races— such as giants—had been mighty and without equal in their own ways. It was difficult to imagine that they had simply just died out.

That said, maybe the giants hadn't had it quite as bad. After all, if the rumors were true, they were still around if you knew where to look. You wouldn't run into one in town, but there had been sightings of them in uncharted territory before, in places difficult for humans to access, such as deep within forests or intensely hot volcanic regions.

What's more, apparently some long-lived races—such as the elves—still had dealings with the giants. It was these sources that had given rise to the rumors of the race's continued existence. Somewhere, out there in the world, the giants still lived. Still, the chances of actually meeting one like this were basically zero. In the first place...

"Are you sure he's a *real* giant?" I asked Lorraine.

"No," she replied, sounding unsure of herself. "Although, he does look like one. He could also just have the ability to turn into a giant, or perhaps he's a giant disguising himself as a human. Actually, I'm not even sure if giants can possess such abilities. I can't say *anything* for certain. I suppose we'll have to ask the person himself."

She was right; it could've been either of those possibilities. Unique abilities were still poorly understood. Nobody knew why they manifested in the specific people they did, or even if they were a strictly human phenomenon. Who knew whether a giant could've had one? It wasn't like it was possible to round up enough giants to get a decent sample size and research it. While that might've been doable in the past, time only ever moved forward.

"He doesn't seem to be in a very talkative mood right now," Augurey joked.

The giant before us was huge. Instead of the skinny old man he'd been before, he looked closer to middle-aged and extremely well-built. Was this his original form, or was it just his ability making him seem younger?

The giant was wearing only a single loincloth. I said a silent prayer of gratitude that he wasn't naked. That would've been distracting in all kinds of ways. Upon closer inspection, I realized that the loincloth was made of the same material as the cloak that the old man had been wearing earlier. Maybe it was some special kind of magic item? It was slightly too big to be the cloak itself. It seemed likely that the cloth could change size to a certain degree as its wearer gigantified himself.

A thought occurred to me, and I looked at the arm that I'd inflicted a wound on earlier. It was still bound up tight, just like it'd been when the old man had been human-sized, which meant the bandages had grown bigger too. That supported my theory about his cloth itself being special in some way.

I guess he could've just left his arm small and gigantified the rest of himself, but for some reason, that picture just didn't seem right in my head—not that my personal thoughts on it mattered. Plus, choosing to do that would've made it harder for him to maintain his balance—not a smart decision for sure.

That aside, how were we going to fight him? It probably would've been an exaggeration to say that I was familiar with fighting huge opponents, but I *did* have experience against giant skeletons and tarasques—monsters that were way bigger than me. As such, size alone wasn't enough to make me falter. On the other hand, those monsters had possessed obvious weaknesses, and I'd gone into those fights with a pretty decent advantage. Comparing them to my current opponent would be just plain silly.

Winning a fight was a lot easier said than done. To begin with, regular sword strikes hadn't even worked on the old man when he was human-sized. Maybe a fully charged spirit swing would have done the job, but I'd gone straight to using mana-spirit fusion.

That was probably the way to go from the outset here. I felt like holding back would only bring this fight to an unfortunate early finish. But just as I was planning my attack…

"Here I come!" With a resounding shout, the former-old-guy-currently-a-giant came straight for us. The sound of his voice alone generated enough pressure to send shivers through me. His huge form looked like the embodiment of sheer brute force as it rushed toward us.

"Split up!" I called out. "We can figure out the rest later!"

Lorraine and Augurey were already moving. They probably knew that, against our giant opponent, sticking together would only make us an easy target.

Against an oncoming group of small—well, human-sized—monsters, it wasn't a bad idea to group up, cover different roles, and whittle away at their numbers, but a plan like that here would've just got us literally slapped into the ground. Lorraine might've been able to delay that outcome with a shield spell, but that was the best we could've hoped for.

I could have used Division too, which would've let me make a getaway, but I didn't much like the idea of being the sole survivor. Talk about heavy.

Anyhow, seeing as I had such a unique ability up my sleeve, I figured it fell to me to act as our group's shield, or maybe its decoy. I started focusing mana and spirit into my sword and turned straight toward the giant to divert his attention away from the directions in which Lorraine and Augurey were running. I tried to ignore the fact that I was basically doing my best wild boar impression. It wasn't my fault the situation had demanded it.

I pumped spirit into my entire body, improving my physical ability, and broke into a full-on sprint. My target was one of the giant's legs. Yeah, that would do for now. Robbing him of his mobility would make for a good start. Despite his body having grown so large, his speed hadn't really lessened, which was pretty scary. It looked like air resistance and such had slowed him down a little, of course, but hardly enough to be of any consolation.

I knew I had to keep my wits about me, and I was proven right. As I reached the giant with my sword held aloft, he lifted his leg, then brought it straight down.

*BOOM!*

The sound of the giant's stomp resounded through the surroundings.

The giant's stomp had been ridiculously fast and had covered a large area of ground. Nevertheless, I was fine; it hadn't squished me into a pulp. Although, even if it had, this was me we were talking about. I could've bounced back from that more than a few times. Being a giant definitely gave you an unfair advantage in a fight, but I was the last person who could go around pointing fingers—most people only got a single squishing before they were done. I couldn't get ahead of myself though. I'd only avoided one attack.

"Dodged that, did you? Then how's this?!" The old giant began stomping at me in quick succession. To my annoyance, he wasn't just stamping around like a kid having a tantrum. He was watching me carefully and aiming at where I stood—as well as where he thought I would run to—with scary precision.

Huge monsters that possessed intelligence were always scary, but the old giant went above and beyond that since, for all intents and purposes, he was an actual person—and a pretty seasoned veteran at that. Although people were far smaller than monsters, we'd managed to ensure our survival in this world by being much more intelligent. But here was this old giant, whose size and strength were equal to or larger than that of a monster's, also every bit as smart as a person. "Dangerous" didn't even begin to describe him, but that didn't mean I was just going to give up.

*BOOM!*

A loud stomp reverberated right next to me, and I felt a shock slam into my left arm from the shoulder down before losing all feeling there entirely. Evidently, my perfect series of dodges had come to an end. That said, I barely felt any pain. As far as my body was concerned, this was nothing more than a scratch.

The old giant, however, didn't know that. "Ah, I know a mortal wound when I see one!" Sounding slightly happy, he stopped stomping and swung a fist at me, probably intending to finish me off.

It wasn't that surprising; no matter how big he got, his body was still person-shaped. The ability to cause harm aside, a person's arms were usually way more accurate than their legs.

The fist came straight for me. The old giant was probably sure it was going to hit. That only made sense; not many people could move at their full capacity right after getting their arm crushed from the shoulder down. "Not many" wasn't "none" though. The world was a big place, and a lot of people in it were unbelievable outliers. It should go without saying that I was including myself in that statement.

I waited until the very last moment, then dodged out of the way before the fist hit me.

"What?!" The old giant made to pull his arm back in surprise, but before he could, I jumped onto it.

I didn't stop there though. I ran along it up to his shoulder, my sword grasped tightly in my hand. It probably wasn't hard for him to realize what I was about to do, but that still put him on the back foot in this situation. I swung my sword imbued with mana and spirit at the old giant's face.

*Slash!*

I felt the weight of my strike landing at the same time I heard the sound of it cutting into flesh. I'd landed a hit…but unfortunately, it hadn't connected with my intended target. The old giant's crazy reaction speed hadn't dulled at all. He'd managed to get his hand in the way of my slash before it could hit his face.

"Ngah!" Then, with a half-groan, half-shout, he reached out to grab me with his injured hand.

I couldn't let him catch me, obviously, but I didn't know how to go about getting away. My fastest option was… Well, it was probably just jumping off him. It wasn't like the fall would kill me, after all. And while climbing down was also an option, I got the feeling that he wasn't easygoing enough to just wait for me to do so. Instead,

I steeled my resolve and leaped into the air. The old giant had likely realized that would be my only option, though, and sure enough…

"You're not going anywhere!" he shouted, flinging his hand out toward me.

I would've said that I was scared he was going to catch me, but that would've been a lie. I channeled as much spirit as I could muster into my back. The old giant's hand shot forward and closed around me…but I was already gone, my previously free-falling body having shifted suddenly to the side. That hadn't actually been the direction I'd wanted to go in, but, hey, trying to maintain fine control over what I was doing was hard.

"Wha—?! Get back here!" The giant reached out for me again, but the moment he did…

"Glacies Cometes!"

A massive ball of ice came flying toward the old giant from the side. It wasn't as big as him by any means—just a third of his size— but that was still pretty impressive. It would've taken a mage with a lot of mana to create it.

No matter how strong the old giant was, or how fast he could react, dodging a huge chunk of ice that had appeared out of nowhere would've been a hard ask for anybody. It crashed straight into him and sent him reeling.

"Nice timing," I muttered to myself as I channeled spirit into my back again. This time, I was trying to land on the ground. Maybe it was because I was able to take things slower while the old giant was recovering his balance, but my control didn't slip, and I successfully headed for my intended destination.

That's right; I was flying. If someone else had been looking at me, they would've seen bat-like wings sprouting out of my back. If I channeled mana into my wings, they'd help me float, whereas if I channeled spirit into them, it gave me a difficult-to-control form of propulsion…and that was pretty much it.

Since they were hard to use, I normally avoided bringing them out in combat, but this was the perfect time for them to shine. They had, after all, helped me avoid the old giant catching and crushing me, and it was thanks to them that I'd get to feel the sweet, sweet sensation of the ground beneath my feet again.

Only one teensy problem remained: the ground in question was currently coming straight at me at a pretty menacing rate.

Like I said before, my wings were difficult to control, so even though I'd somehow got myself going in the right direction, it didn't look like a soft landing was going to be in my future.

"Hrngf!"

My awkward landing, by which I mean my collision with the ground, forced a weird grunt out of me. I stood up right away and dashed for a section of the surrounding woods that the old giant hadn't torn up yet. We were close to the village, meaning people used this area of the woods, so there was enough space between the trees to move about, and it wouldn't be too hard to get my bearings once I was deeper in either.

But it was a different story for the old giant. He was taller than the trees themselves. From his point of view, it would just look like a sea of foliage. It would be hard for him to find us underneath it.

The old giant was strong and fast enough to seem like an unbeatable opponent, but his size came with some unexpected disadvantages. Still, he probably knew that already and had ways to deal with them. He didn't seem like the type to overlook that kind of thing.

"Clever! But I can still see you!"

The old giant began swiping his fists in the direction I was running. Apparently, he couldn't see me as well as he claimed, though, because his aim was worse than it had been before. Still, since his attacks were so wide-reaching to begin with, a lot of the swipes were closer calls than I would've liked.

As I was running around wondering what I should do next, I caught a sudden glance of Augurey to my flank.

"Rentt!" he shouted, dashing over to run by my side.

Although the sound of the old giant's fists crashing through the trees was much louder, I'd still managed to hear Augurey's shout.

"Augurey! What's wrong?!"

"Lorraine said the only way we're winning this is if we hit him hard! *Really* hard!"

Evidently, Augurey had come by to fill me in on our battle plan. After thinking about it, I realized Lorraine had made the right call. My chipping away at the old giant was making *some* progress, but at the end of the day, I was only scratching him. I hadn't been able to convert any of my hits into a finishing blow.

My mana and spirit weren't limitless either. I had already put a decent amount of my strength into my sword—the only thing that had gotten me past the old giant's sheer durability. He really wasn't making this easy.

"But how?!" I yelled. "It's not like we can just plop her in front of him!"

"We have to bait him somewhere where she can land a spell on him! Just like we did with the aqua hatul!"

The aqua hatul, huh? Back then, we'd caught it by chasing it to a spot where Lorraine had laid a trap in the form of a magical cage. Doing the same with the old giant would be impossible, obviously, but I supposed Augurey meant that we should get *him* to chase *us*. I figured that was definitely doable, given that we were *already* doing it.

"Where?!" I asked.

"This way!" Augurey shouted, running forward and taking the lead. He was as fast as you might expect of somebody who was Silver-class. He'd enhanced his body, but it had probably been with spirit and not magic.

It was one thing if you had the mana to spare, but if you were picking between the two, then spirit offered you more stamina. For adventurers, it was a favorite among the warrior types. All the same, spellblades and such had their own methods, and... Well, whatever, you get the idea.

Anyway, Augurey and I ran. We had an old giant on our tail, and we needed to lead him into a trap.

"They're here!"

Lorraine could see the giant advancing through the woods toward her, crashing through the trees and uprooting them like a destructive tornado. His sheer size had invoked an instinctual kind of fear inside her when she'd seen him up close earlier, but seeing him from far away was scary too in its own way. When she thought about how giants had been much more common in bygone eras and how they'd probably menaced humans at times, it made her wonder how the latter had even survived to flourish today.

That said, she could ponder the past later. Right now, there was only one thing she needed to do: conjure up an attack powerful enough to take the giant out.

In order to give herself the clearest shot at her target, Lorraine had asked Augurey to tell Rentt to "bait the giant somewhere where I can hit him in the flank with a spell." It seemed Augurey had done his job, because the old giant was heading in the exact direction they'd planned for.

All that was left was to mold her mana, construct her spell, and fire it, but that was easier said than done. Not even Lorraine had an inexhaustible supply of mana. It didn't help that she'd probably dipped into it more than necessary with the Glacies Cometes she'd cast earlier. The spell wasn't originally supposed to create a ball of ice that large—it had just ended up that way because she'd cobbled it together with brute force. She still had mana to work with, of course, but not enough that she was fully reassured regarding what she was about to do.

Be that as it may, it wasn't like she had a choice. A cloud of dust was steadily approaching. Rentt and Augurey were probably just under the giant, running like crazy. If she failed, it'd be the end for all of them. She couldn't let that happen.

Lorraine began molding her mana. Since she didn't know what kind of abilities the old giant possessed, she did so as carefully as she could, to avoid his notice. It took her more time than it usually would have, but she had a rough estimate of her target's speed and distance. So long as she stayed calm, everything would be fine. And then the time came.

"Lorraine!"

She heard Rentt's voice. It hadn't been that loud; in fact, the sound of the giant destroying the surroundings had almost drowned it out. Still, Lorraine had heard it. It would've been impossible for her to miss. Her eyes flashed open, and the moment the old giant stepped into the spot she'd picked, she recited her chant.

"Terra Cavus!"

A vast amount of mana aggregated around the old giant's feet, creating a loud *boom* as it caved in the surrounding earth. The hole was big enough to fit the old giant's entire body. The sudden lack of footing caused him to fall, but he quickly began to pick himself back up. However, Lorraine wasn't finished.

"Not yet! Yiesh Gadólmagén!"

A large number of sizable metal lances formed into existence, each one packed with a potent amount of mana that enhanced its strength. The moment they fully manifested, they shot straight for the fallen giant.

The old giant's skin was tough enough to repel one of Rentt's spirit-charged sword strikes, but Lorraine hadn't held back from packing her lances full of mana, giving them a significant amount of destructive power. Nonetheless, although they pierced the old giant's body, they did so with difficulty, and none of the wounds they caused seemed serious. His sheer sturdiness was impressive.

"And now, finally... Hazina Barqrasūl!"

In the blink of an eye, swirling black clouds formed in the sky, from which shot forth a colossal thunderbolt. It struck the old giant with a deafening *crack*, and the light it gave off turned the surroundings a pure, blinding white.

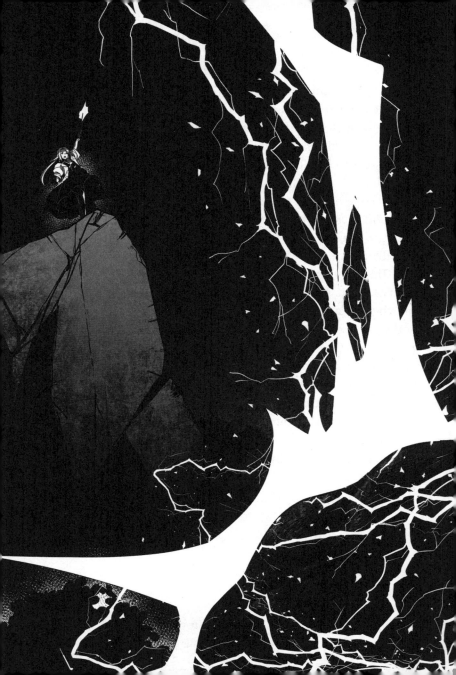

The area was filled with the reek of burnt flesh and the unique, stimulating odor that lingered after a lightning strike. Coupled with all of the dust in the air, it was pretty unpleasant. That aside, it seemed like Lorraine's spells had worked. There were probably beings out there who *could* have endured that onslaught, but I felt fairly certain there weren't very many.

"That was...ridiculous," Augurey said. The two of us had barely made it out of the range of Lorraine's spells and seen it all up close.

If *I'd* been hit by that, I had a feeling that not even my undead body could have avoided being obliterated. And while I didn't feel pain, evidently I did still feel fear, because my instincts were telling me that if that thunderbolt had hit me, I would have been gone for good. Did that mean I was alive, even though I was undead? The meaning of life and other similarly philosophical questions were on the verge of getting loose and spinning around in my head, but I tamped them down. Now wasn't the time.

"They do say an experienced mage is worth an entire army," I said. "And after seeing that, I can understand why."

"An army, huh?" Augurey replied. "Something tells me just one wouldn't have been enough. I'd never seen any of those spells before."

"Lorraine knows a decent amount of ancient spells. I wouldn't be surprised if those were all examples. She said she doesn't use them much since they take a lot of mana, but I guess even if they didn't, they wouldn't be the kind of magic you'd use every day anyhow."

The old giant had smashed, crushed, and uprooted a sizable chunk of the woods, but Lorraine had been no slouch herself when it came to the sheer amount of destruction caused.

I'd been treating the old giant like a monster, but apparently we'd had another monster in our party this whole time. Make that two, actually; I couldn't forget to count myself. Wait, did that mean Augurey was the only normal person? I felt kind of guilty all of a sudden. Well, whatever. It had been *his* requests that had led to all this. I figured that made us even.

"Still, you think that was enough?" Augurey asked, his expression grim. "I mean, I'd be surprised if it wasn't, but..."

He was looking at the old giant, but the surrounding trees were still smoking from the thunderbolt, so neither of us were able to confirm anything yet. I was fairly sure it was over, but it never hurt to make sure.

The smoke gradually cleared, giving us a view of something massive and burnt—the old giant. He wasn't completely charred all over—probably because he was too big—but a lot of him had been scorched black and brown. The thunderbolt had clearly hit its mark.

I couldn't see any of Lorraine's metal lances, so I figured that they'd run out of mana. The punctures they'd made into the old giant were still there, however, and I could see smoke sputtering out of them. It looked like the thunderbolt had penetrated pretty deep.

Despite the old giant's size and despite how much he defied common sense, at the end of the day, he was still a living being. A powerful thunderbolt passing through his entire body was nothing to sneeze at.

"We got him, right?" Augurey muttered. We were both slowly approaching the old giant. We held our swords aloft, though, ready for the possibility that he'd get up.

Augurey reached the old giant and poked him with the tip of his sword. No response.

"Looks like we did," Augurey said, turning back to me. "Thank goodness for that."

But just as he was breathing a sigh of relief…

"Augurey!" I yelled.

With a rush of wind, the old giant's arm swung out wide. I grabbed Augurey and jumped back, quickly making some distance.

"Grrraaahhh!" The old giant let out a half-human, half-bestial cry, and began to slowly sit up. He placed his hand on the ground, and with a hard push, made to stand.

"You're kidding me!" Augurey said. He was still in my arms, watching the old giant.

I couldn't blame him for being shocked; I was too. "Incredible" didn't even begin to describe the amount of endurance and toughness it would take to stand up after eating a spell onslaught like that. The old giant was a monster who broke all the rules, pure and simple.

"It hurt him though," I said, letting Augurey down. "That's for sure."

Observing the old giant calmly, I could tell that his movements were definitely duller. I could hear his joints cracking too as he made to stand. Lorraine's thunderbolt had done a lot of damage.

Finally, the old giant rose to his feet. A pair of bloodshot eyes on a scorched face focused on Augurey and me, and with a snarl, he came straight for us. All traces of his former composure were gone.

"Augurey! Can you keep going?!" I shouted.

"I can do this all day! The only problem is, how are we going to bring him down?"

"I'll do it. I've got a trump card I can use. I don't know if my sword can handle doing it more than once though, so if I miss, we're done for."

The old giant had started his assault on us already, so we were calling out to each other as we dodged. The "trump card," I was talking about was divinity-mana-spirit fusion. Although my sword had been forged to withstand any of the three, it probably couldn't resist all of them together.

The technique caused anything it hit to violently crumple in on itself, and it was likely that the same would happen to my sword. That was why I wanted to avoid using it as much as possible, but if *now* wasn't the right time, then I didn't know what was. There was a chance it wouldn't even work, or that it wouldn't be enough to be a finishing blow, but it was better than doing nothing and just waiting to lose. If I was going to lose—not that I had any intention of doing so—it would only be after I'd given everything I had. And even then, I was preparing myself to run before I went down.

Escaping hadn't seemed like an option before, but now that the old giant was so injured, the three of us could probably manage it. I doubted he'd chase after us in the state he was in, and I was confident in our ability to get away too.

That raised the problem of Ferrici and the villagers, but I supposed we could always just evacuate them somewhere. Either that or take Goblin and Siren as hostages and try to strike a bargain. It was definitely villainous of me to consider that, but, hey, whatever means necessary.

At any rate, none of that was important compared to what I had to do right now, so it was probably best that I focused on the present.

"All or nothing, huh?" Augurey said. "All right, I don't hate it. I'm the decoy this time, right?"

"Are you sure?" I asked.

"I'll just run if it looks like I'm going to die, so don't blame me if that happens. Besides, I can't let you and Lorraine do *all* the work."

"I'm counting on you, then. But don't overdo it. Unlike me, you can't get crushed and walk away in one piece."

Although, the truth was that I couldn't exactly do that either, given I didn't know how many times it would take before I vanished completely. I could probably guess based on the young vampires I'd encountered in Maalt, but that was far from being a sure thing.

Long story short, the danger was mutual. Augurey and I would just have to do the best we could. We steeled ourselves for the task at hand—not that we hadn't been ready before.

"Hey! Over here!" Augurey shouted. True to what he'd just told me, he'd deliberately run out right in front of the old giant to act as a decoy.

The problem was whether our opponent would take the bait, but I'd figured that if he couldn't see me, he'd have no choice but to go for the only visible target. Therefore, I used Division and hid myself in the shadows of the woods to ensure he focused his attention on Augurey.

If anybody saw me in this state, unless they were clued in on what I was, they'd think of me as nothing more than a patch of shadow. Although the old giant probably had some idea that I wasn't normal, I doubted that he'd figured out enough about me to know I could turn myself into darkness.

I was proven right. The old giant glanced my way for a moment, but it didn't seem like he'd noticed me, because he soon switched his focus back to Augurey and began moving away. He might even have been suspecting some kind of trap, but he'd been left with no choice anyway.

I was worried about how well Augurey would hold out, but to my surprise, he was doing just fine. The fact that his combat style focused on speed instead of power was paying off. Part of it was that his opponent's movements had dulled considerably, but Augurey was dodging the old giant's attacks with room to spare. Of course, that did nothing to detract from the danger Augurey was in, since all it would take was one slipup for him to suffer a serious injury—or even possibly die.

The sooner I took the old giant down, the better. I thought about where I should aim my strike and came to the conclusion that going for the head was probably my best bet. The old giant had already proven that his arms and legs could take a beating and still keep going. In that case, how was I going to reach his head? I considered using my wings to fly up, but that was too risky. I only had one chance at this; I couldn't waste it on something so uncertain. I had to think of something else—

"Ah!"

But before I could, I saw Augurey's foot catch against the root of a tree.

The old giant's fist swung at Augurey, but before it could connect, I dashed out, grabbed my friend, and ran to the side... where I realized my way was blocked by trees.

Left with no other option, I jumped as hard as I could. The old giant's arm passed below me, only barely missing, and I landed atop it as it went by. But just as the old giant's attention was about to focus on me, I heard the sound of a chant.

"Gadól Barák!"

A thick bolt of lightning struck the old giant. It had come from Lorraine. Clearly, she could still manage spells like this even after the grand onslaught she'd cast earlier.

A crackling sound rang in my ears as some of the lightning passed through the old giant and into me, but otherwise, I was mostly unaffected. I could still move. I didn't have my monster body to thank this time; it was my robe that had done the job.

That being said, I *had* started to go a little numb, and I was pretty sure that being on the receiving end of any more would be a bad idea. I leaped off the old giant while he was busy recoiling from the lightning and once again hid in the trees.

I dropped Augurey off, and then, noticing that the only sound he was making was incoherent babbling, healed him up with a little bit of divinity.

"Wow, that spell did a number on me," he said. "Sorry. I didn't get the job done."

I didn't think that was true, given his performance out there. On top of that, it had just given me an idea. It was relatively simple, but I thought it had a chance of working out. I told Augurey, and he nodded.

"That...might just work. I mean, it's not too different from what you just did. Well, it's still crazy, but this is *you* we're talking about."

And so I had Augurey's approval.

The two of us went out to take on the old giant again. Augurey, just like earlier, ran out in front and began dodging his attacks. Meanwhile, I kept a close eye on him, waiting for the perfect time...

*Now!*

I broke into the fastest sprint I could manage. The old giant had thrown a punch, and as a result, he was slightly hunched over. The slight angle between his legs and head meant that his back was a steep slope.

That's right, *slope*. I jumped on. After seeing me do so, Augurey dodged out of the way of the punch without a moment to spare and fell back.

"Hmm?!" The old giant tried to stand up straight immediately.

Fortunately, I had already reached my destination: the back of his neck. It was a vital part of the body for any living creature, as well as the most vulnerable blind spot, and although some creatures were extraordinarily tough or had sharp thorns or similar defenses, a giant's body was basically the same as a human's, just bigger and sturdier.

In short, their vital organs and weak points were in the same places too, so the back of the old giant's neck was the perfect spot for me to strike. Probably. Whatever the case, I was already committed. If this didn't work, I'd just resort to my next best plan: beating a hasty retreat. As for the time being, I channeled all of my mana, divinity, and spirit into my sword and swung it as hard as I could.

The old giant was too injured to react in time. He failed to guard against my strike. It connected directly with the back of his neck, and despite the fact that I was now in a free fall through the air, I had a clear view of his flesh as it immediately began to crumple.

Then I saw a spray of blood burst forth from the old giant's neck, accompanied by the sound of something rupturing.

"All right!" I struck a victory pose midair...then realized what was about to happen. "Wait, no, crap!"

But it was already too late. The old giant slumped limply forward and began to collapse in the same direction I was falling. It didn't take a genius to figure out that I was about to be turned into paste, and given the situation, it didn't seem likely that I was going to get a timely rescue. Well, at least I was fairly sure that I wasn't going to die.

Channeling spirit into my wings might've saved me, but unfortunately, I'd just used up every last drop of strength I had. While another ten seconds probably would've been enough for me to recover enough spirit to channel, I'd definitely be crushed before then.

I prayed that I wasn't on my final squishing. I was, of course, talking about using Division to recover. I *thought* I could still manage it, but I couldn't say for sure.

Then, with a loud *smack*, I was crushed. And I mean it—no doubts, no last-minute dodges, nothing. I was really crushed to a pulp.

Reconstructing my body from pulp felt kind of strange. I used Division to temporarily become a mass of shadow, then formed myself back into my original shape. The expressions on Lorraine and Augurey's faces as they watched me return looking none the worse for wear were difficult to read.

"I already knew you weren't human anymore, but that really puts it into perspective," Lorraine said.

"That's a pretty unfair trick," Augurey added. "Remind me never to pick a fight with you, Rentt. How's a guy supposed to beat that? At least with giants it feels like you have a chance because you can tell that you're slowly chipping away at them."

I thought those were pretty awful things to say.

"It's not like I can take an infinite amount of punishment," I said. "Even I'd die at some point. Probably."

I didn't have the experience to back that up, but I *had* seen it happen to others before. It was a sad way to go out, and one I wanted to avoid. If I was going to die, I wanted it to be while I was at peace in bed. Then again, that was probably too much to ask for considering I was an adventurer, so I'd settle for any kind of decent death. Absentmindedly fading out of existence was just too half-baked. Did that even count as dying?

That said, I probably didn't have the right to be picky since I'd already died once. Maybe it was fine if round two ended up being kind of a throwaway. The only thing was, I couldn't really remember much about what my first death felt like. I'd have to make sure to commit my second one to memory if it was the last thing I ever did... which it would be.

But that was enough joking around for the time being.

"Now this is a surprise," I said. "He looks so small now."

I was looking at the old giant, who was now back to being a skinny old man. He was lying in the hole made by his larger self's fall, his cloth draped over him. The sight was kind of sad and lonely, actually.

You didn't really hear of it happening around these parts, but sometimes poverty-stricken villages and such would abandon their elderly in the woods once they'd reached a certain age. I'd come across them several times on trips out to the countryside, and it was always rough to see. I couldn't just leave them, of course, so I'd always tell them to come with me. Returning to their home villages obviously hadn't been an option, so I'd helped them find a place where they could earn themselves a living—which hadn't been too difficult, actually. Turns out all you needed to do was look in the right places.

I doubted the old man lying in front of me needed to worry about that though. You could probably toss him in any old tavern and he'd easily earn his own keep by arm wrestling people and betting on it. A knightly order or the military would work too, and he'd definitely do fine as an adventurer.

I wondered why he'd picked this cloak-and-dagger business instead. Maybe the pay was good? To be honest, I had no idea.

"I think we can safely assume that his gigantification was due to some kind of special ability," Lorraine said. "That would explain why it reverted after he lost consciousness."

She was probably right; I couldn't think of any better explanations.

"We can leave that for later." Augurey shook his head. He sounded astonished. "I can't believe it, but I think he's still alive."

It was easy to understand how Augurey felt. To have taken a beating like that and survived? The old man's sheer durability was astounding.

Upon closer inspection, I noticed that the wound I'd made on his neck was still there, but it was a lot smaller than I'd thought it would be. It was clearly bleeding, but you couldn't really call it a fatal injury. He'd likely gone down because my divinity-mana-spirit fusion strike had hit him hard in the back of the neck...which probably meant that I had been cutting it real close back there. Any other outcome probably would've ended with *me* lying in the dirt.

"Should we finish him off?" I asked. "We're done for if he wakes up and gigantifies again."

"You're right, but I want to hear what he has to say," Lorraine said. "We still don't know exactly why we're being targeted. Although, I do have a decent idea."

I did too. It wasn't that hard to connect the dots. This had all happened right after we'd met the princess, so the person who'd sent the assassins after us was most assumably one of her enemies. Chances were it was one of her royal siblings or their supporters.

Still, that was the extent of what I could deduce. Lorraine was right about wanting the specifics. Our future options hinged on having that information. The princess would probably want to hear it too, so perhaps that could give us some breathing room in our negotiations with her.

"So...what now?" I asked. "Should we cut him up so he can't move?"

I knew it was a pretty horrifying suggestion to make, but that just went to show how strong the old man was. If we left him alive, it would be hard to keep him in check. I wasn't sure we had any other option.

Augurey's face lit up like he'd suddenly remembered something. "Oh, how about this? I figured they might come in handy at some point, so I kept some on me. I know you can't usually force a person into one, but we've got Lorraine with us. You think it'll work?"

He pulled a familiar-looking set of documents out of his bag.

"A magic contract, huh?" I said. "That's not a bad idea. You're right that we'd usually need the person's consent, but we could probably trick a contract of this quality."

I made it sound simple, but it was a feat only possible because we had Lorraine. Your average mage wouldn't know how, and even if they tried, it'd take them a lot of effort.

On top of that, magic contracts came in varying qualities to suit the occasion. The better one was, the harder it was to meddle with. Anyhow, it was convenient that the option was open to us.

"Should we restrict him from using his ability without our permission?" I asked. "He's stupidly strong even without it though. What do we do if he gets out of control?"

"Make it so he dies if he does that," Lorraine replied.

There was a pause.

"That was a joke," she said. "It's not a terrible option, but it's not really a clean one either. It'd be hard for a magic contract of this quality to enforce that in the first place. We'd need a potent one from a temple of Hozei for that. The best this will let us do is restrict his ability. Even then, chances are high it'll break easily, since we don't have his consent. It didn't seem as if he could do much magic, though, so I'll just restrict his mana usage."

Lorraine sounded disappointed as she explained things while quickly drafting the contract. After she finished, she began casting some kind of suspicious spell on the old man...

Just kidding. She was doing exactly what she'd said she would: setting up a field that temporarily prevented the use of magic. A magic contract was a type of *magic* item, so if you wanted to break the agreement that it dictated, you needed to use magic too.

The final issue was getting his signature, but just because he was unconscious didn't mean we couldn't get it. In fact, as far as magic contracts were concerned, a thumbprint was fine too. Most people didn't do it, because you'd have to make a small cut and use some of your own blood, but given the circumstances we were in...

In the first place, Lorraine was doing all the work of tricking the contract. All I had to do was cap it off by pressing the old man's thumb to it.

I made a small nick on this thumb, which actually took some effort. What was his skin made of? Rock? At any rate, I pressed it to the contract. I decided to be the other party, which meant that my consent would be necessary to annul it later on. I didn't have any terms forced on me though, so in that sense, it differed from general business contracts. That was why it had been given its own unique term, "magic contract," and... Whatever. Now wasn't the time to get into all that.

I signed my name on the contract and Lorraine muttered some kind of spell over it. From the way it glowed, I could tell it had successfully been completed. Now we just had to pray that he wouldn't gigantify when he woke up. More accurately, the hope was that nothing would happen even if he did.

Either way, that took care of that problem. We could explain the contract to him after he calmed down. The only issue would be whether he'd talk to us, but Lorraine had also added a few detailed clauses that would prevent him from doing things like lying to us. She was thorough like that. The only thing left to do now was to wait for him to wake up.

After a while had passed...

"Ngh..."

The old man shook his head and opened his eyes. Surprisingly, he didn't lash out immediately. Instead, he took the time to examine his surroundings. After looking at each of us in turn, he sighed.

"You're not going to gigantify?" I asked. I hadn't meant to, but the question had slipped from my mouth.

The old man shook his head. "I'm not sure how long I was out, but I'm sure you came up with a countermeasure for that. There's no other explanation for why I'm still alive. I won't waste the effort."

I was impressed that he'd grasped the situation already.

"Thanks for saving us the time," Lorraine said. "I'll give you the specifics, then. We've made it so that you can't gigantify without our permission. You can't lie to us either. Why don't you try it out?"

He proceeded to do just that by tensing up, although where exactly, I couldn't tell.

"Hrng…!"

We still didn't know how he activated his ability, but evidently he triggered it by focusing power somewhere. On the other hand, his tensing up could just be a habit with little meaning.

Nevertheless, he seemed to reach the conclusion that we'd told him the truth. He sighed again.

"You're right. I can't. I'm no better than any other old man now. Don't suppose you could undo these bindings, could you?"

Lorraine had cast magical bindings on him to restrict his movements. Apparently, he wanted them off.

"With all due respect," Augurey replied, "your brute strength is really nothing to sneeze at, even at this size. You'd pick a fight as soon as we undid them. So, no."

I figured Augurey was right and that was exactly what the old man was after.

"Goodness me." The old man sniffed, proving us right. "You couldn't have let your guard down even a little bit?"

We really couldn't have, not against someone as sharp as him. Fortunately, not even he could do much in this situation, and it seemed like he knew that.

The old man glanced around at us. "So? You've got me bound and alive. I'm guessing that means you have questions for me. Ask them."

You'd think he had *us* captive with how haughty he was, but I could kind of understand his defiance, seeing as how thoroughly bound up he was.

"It's always something unexpected with you, isn't it?" Lorraine said. "Well, whatever. I'll get straight to the point. Why did you come after us? And I'm including Goblin and Siren as part of that."

"Straight to the point indeed," the old man replied. "But I'm not obligated to talk... Ah, no, looks like I can't get away with staying silent. The reason's simple. The second princess summoned you to meet with her. That's that."

From the look of things, the old man had tried keeping his mouth shut to avoid being forced to tell us the truth, but it hadn't worked out—he was coming clean with us. I'd heard that trying to resist "no lying" or "no staying silent" clauses in magic contracts made you feel restless and itchy, and your mouth would end up speaking even if you didn't want it to. I hadn't experienced it for myself, though. I kind of wanted to try it once, but seeing as how that would probably only happen if I landed myself in deep trouble of some kind, I thought better of it.

At any rate, the old man had given us the exact reason we'd been expecting.

Lorraine sighed. "I knew it but was that really all it took? To be frank with you, all we did was make small talk and drink tea. Surely that shouldn't qualify us as a target for monsters like you."

Lorraine wasn't *wrong*, exactly. That was pretty much what had actually happened, if you left out the specifics. Just because we were questioning the old man didn't mean we had to give him any information to work with, especially since he seemed perceptive enough to make good guesses from even small tidbits. That was probably why Lorraine had phrased her words the way she had—to give him as little information as possible. But the old man's reply was unexpected.

"I understand why you'd want to play dumb, but we more or less already know what you talked about with the second princess. The scepter of the kingdom, no? His Majesty's current condition too."

"What are you talking about?" Lorraine asked.

"Don't bother," the old man replied. "If we hadn't known *that* much, we wouldn't be here in the first place. And considering your capabilities, I'd guess she probably ordered you to go and retrieve the new scepter. She did well to find you though; I'll give her that. I was convinced we'd suppressed all of her standout options already."

The old man had pretty much hit the mark, but he was still a little off. It sounded like he didn't know that, while the princess *had* asked us to go fetch the new scepter, in the end, it had turned into more of a conditional thing. Technically, we didn't have any orders right now. He also didn't seem to know about the prophecy she'd told us about.

Even so, how had he found out? I didn't think there had been any spying magic items in the room. The princess would have accounted for that kind of thing. Even if she hadn't, Lorraine would've noticed. Given her next question, though, it seemed like Lorraine had figured something out from the old man's information.

"You hired a diviner, didn't you? They must have been pretty good too."

"Ho! You're sharp. Yes, from what I heard, they've never got anything wrong. We actually had them look into my past as a test, and they were able to give very specific answers. Some of which were…a little off, actually. In any case, it *was* obvious that you three were too dangerous to leave alive. That was why we were ordered to kill you."

Similar to how the high elves had given the princess a prophecy, people called diviners could see into the past and future. Some were genuinely accurate too. However, since it was pretty hard to discern truth from lies with that kind of thing, most of them were considered to be scam artists. Nonetheless, taking into account the old man's explanation, his employer had succeeded in hiring a real diviner. Talk about getting lucky.

Still, I wondered why they weren't aware of the most important details. Even the diviner must have been curious. They must have looked into it, right? Either way, thinking about it wouldn't get me anywhere.

Although…there *were* folktales about that kind of thing— gods interfering with divination and stuff like that. And this whole affair involved the high elves' prophecy, meaning it involved the Holy Tree, which was apparently close to being a god itself. Maybe that was why the divination had been kind of shortsighted.

Lorraine then asked the most important question of all.

"So, who was it that gave you those orders?"

"The first princess, Her Royal Highness Nadia Regina Yaaran," the old man said. "But, no, not quite. Her Royal Highness isn't actually aware of these matters."

Lorraine pressed deeper. "Then who *is* the ringleader?"

"Need you even ask? Countess Gisel Georgiou—Her Royal Highness's greatest backer. She's a valiant woman who wants the first princess to one day succeed the throne."

"That makes sense," Lorraine said.

It sounded like our guesses about the first princess had been correct. She—well, her followers really, which made things messier—had targeted us because we'd developed a connection with the second princess, and that had turned us into a problem.

If it had been the first princess herself, we could have reported this attack to the second princess, which might have given her a basis upon which to denounce her sister, but since it was only a backer...

All the same, it would lead to ramifications, of course, but I doubted it would be enough to topple the first princess herself.

That kind of detailed political maneuvering wasn't in our wheelhouse anyway—we were adventurers. Letting the second princess know and wishing her luck was probably the way to go, except I didn't especially want to paint another target on our backs. I couldn't really think of a good solution.

Still, royalty sure had it rough. Having to scheme around your own family like that was... Wait, was that even the case here? The first princess hadn't actually come up with this plan. I wasn't sure how good a relationship she had with her sister either. I'd assumed that if anybody was out to get the second princess, it would be the first prince or first princess, but truth be told, I had no idea how they felt about each other. Maybe I'd ask the next time I got the chance.

"In short, your employer is Countess Gisel Georgiou?" Lorraine asked.

The old man nodded. "Although, technically, that isn't quite right either. It's true that she hired Goblin, Siren, and me, but we actually belong to an organization, which sold our services to her for a certain period of time."

"Organization?"

"Yes. One made up of people with unique or special abilities like us. We're dispatched to all kinds of jobs depending on what's needed. This was one of them."

Augurey's eyes went wide in surprise. "I never would've guessed a group like that existed…"

The old man smiled. "You might already know this, but we ability wielders aren't exactly celebrated. It's the same story everywhere you go. Rural villages are even worse with how they treat us. Being driven out is the best we can hope for; sometimes they even kill us. The organization rescues such people, raises them into fully-fledged assassins, and gives them work. It's a charity, really. Not a bad deal, no? I'm sure my fellow monster there understands."

He'd directed that last part at me. A monster, huh? Ouch. From the sound of it, he'd mistaken me for another ability wielder, which was understandable. It'd be hard for anyone to tell that I was actually a *monster*-monster without an up close examination. If they did find out, I'd have to dispose of them.

I decided to let the old man remain mistaken. All the same, who could've guessed an organization like that existed? The world sure was a big place, which was probably how *I* would make others feel too, if they knew about me. Besides, even though the old man's premise was mistaken, I got what he was saying.

People with strange abilities were unwelcome and excluded. In other words, they were treated with the same fear that I'd felt from others during my time as a skeleton and ghoul. If people could tell you were different at a glance, then you were already fighting an uphill battle for their approval.

You'd get accused of being different, you'd be driven away, and you'd be kept out. In a sense, those instincts were how the weak maintained and protected their place in this world, but to their even weaker victims, it would only feel like everything and everyone had abandoned them.

I had been lucky; I'd had Lorraine, Rina, Sheila, and even Augurey—kindhearted people who'd accepted me even when I became a monster.

But if I hadn't had them, then in all likelihood, I would've ended up as nothing more than a genuine monster in heart *and* body. Wandering in the wilderness away from society, killing and eating people—just thinking about it scared me. I understand why an organization like the one the old man had described would seem like a source of salvation to ability wielders.

It was also a terrifying opponent to go up against. If the old man was anything to go by, then ability wielders were *scary*. If people like him came after me all the time, I'd need a lot more lives.

Lorraine, Augurey, and I, after some consideration, decided to consult each other about what the old man had said. To prevent him from hearing us, Lorraine set up a barrier.

"Any ideas about what we should do?" she asked. "We know who our enemies are now, but…"

"Well, first things first. How about we ask if he can get them to back off?" Augurey suggested.

I thought that was being too optimistic, personally, but there wasn't any harm in trying.

"Why not?" I said. "If it works, great. If it doesn't, we'll figure out what to do from there."

Lorraine nodded. "I suppose. We also have the option of going to the countess and this 'organization' to speak with them directly. Although, it would be fairly risky."

I wanted to avoid a place filled with people like the old man as much as humanly possible, but I couldn't deny that we'd probably have to go eventually. Asking the second princess to make amends with—or at least do something about—her older sister was an option too, but I had no idea if that was even possible.

"I guess we start with the easiest and work our way up," I said, marking the end of our group discussion.

Lorraine dropped her barrier and turned to the old man. "I'm aware that I might be asking for the impossible, but could you call your people off us? Or, if you don't personally have the authority to do that, could you arrange a meeting for us with someone who can?"

That would probably end up being the countess or the organization's leader, both of which seemed like pretty far-fetched options.

But after some consideration, the old man said, "Hmm. Why not? I'm a dead man as it stands anyway."

Despite being the ones who'd asked, we were kind of surprised.

"I know it was our idea, but is this really okay?" Lorraine asked as we walked.

We'd more or less come to an agreement, but it was still kind of hard to believe. It was also a little suspicious how quickly the old man had accepted our request.

As for where we were walking to, we were on our way back to Ferrici. And if you were wondering, the old man was still bound up with magic. He could only move his legs.

It was reassuring knowing that he couldn't gigantify anymore, but his base physical ability was still amazing in its own right. We were making him walk in front of us and were ready to react the moment he did anything fishy.

To paint a picture of the scene, a guy in a skull mask, a shady mage, and a gaudy show-off had ordered a bound old man to walk in front of them and were keeping an eye on him from behind. I was convinced people would think we were slave traders or something if they saw us. To be fair, the old man did seem like he'd sell for a lot. If we decided to use this opportunity to make a career switch, we could probably make a killing.

"I said as much earlier, but odds are I'm already dead," the old man said. "It'd be obvious to anybody that I botched the job. I can't exactly waltz right back like nothing happened. I suppose I *could* go on the run, but the other two would never last if they did the same."

"Do you mean Goblin and Siren?" I asked. "I guess you're right. They didn't really seem like they knew their way around a fight."

"Come to think of it, I know this is rather late of me now, but is Siren all right?" the old man asked. "I thought there was a chance you might've killed her."

He looked relaxed; his shoulders were loose as he walked. Despite that, his nerve in the face of the situation made it clear he was someone you could never underestimate.

Not for the first time, I found myself amazed by him. While I didn't want to give him any information, I figured it would probably be fine if I told him his colleague was okay. After talking with him so much, I could tell that he was the type who really cared about his allies. Maybe that mindset stemmed from the way the world treated ability wielders.

Everybody got lonely when left to their own devices. Back when I had been stuck in the dungeon, I'd sometimes worried if I would be alone forever. I didn't like to think back on those times much.

I exchanged looks with Lorraine and Augurey, and we all seemed to agree that it would be okay to answer the old man.

"She's fine," Augurey said. "We didn't torture her or anything. Er… We didn't, right?"

He'd directed that last uneasy part at Lorraine. She'd been the one who'd questioned Siren, and we weren't sure how she'd done it. It wasn't *completely* impossible that she'd done some pretty horrible things to force a confession.

"Not at all," Lorraine replied. "I can't really say I injured her in any physical way, and her mind is fine too. I can assure you that her sense of self is the same as it always was."

I thought that was kind of a suspicious way to phrase it, but I could probably take it to mean that Siren was fine. Right? Right. I hoped so, at least.

The old man didn't seem particularly concerned. Instead, he breathed a rare sigh of relief. "I see. That's good." Then, after a moment, he added, "I told you I'd take you to my employer earlier, yes?"

"*Please* don't tell me you're backing out of that now," I said. Just thinking about the kind of mess we'd have to deal with if he did that exhausted me, and that probably came through in my tone.

The old man smiled. "Relax. I'll keep my word. But we do need a way of getting in touch. I'd like to have Goblin and Siren act as messengers."

Oh, he was talking about how we were going to do this. He was probably right too. If we dragged him in by the scruff of the neck and asked to see their boss, it would only break out into a fight then and there. That was probably going to be our last resort anyway, but it was called a *last* resort for a reason. Giving advance notice that we'd be coming was probably a good idea.

"You're right. We do need that," Augurey said. He sounded concerned. "It's just, I'm not sure if we can trust them."

Which was true. It was entirely possible that if we sent either one back as a messenger, it would only result in a group of people as monstrous as the old man coming after us, so we obviously couldn't just smile and nod along with his suggestion. However, it seemed like he'd already taken that into account.

"It's only natural you wouldn't trust us," the old man remarked. "That said, we *do* need a messenger. Would it help a little if you kept one as a hostage and sent the other? Personally, I recommend sending Goblin. I can't be sure Siren won't do something unnecessary. So, how about it?"

Truth be told, we didn't have much in the way of other options. Siren was definitely the overly confident, make-a-name-for-herself type, so there was always the chance she'd abandon the old man and Goblin if we let her go.

I had no idea what the old man would do if we let him go himself, which was scary. And if we sent both Goblin and Siren, then he might just cut and run. The only remaining option was to send Goblin as our messenger and keep the old man and Siren with us as hostages.

"Fine, let's go with that," Lorraine said, after seeing Augurey and me nod. "But you mentioned how risky going back would be. Will he be all right?"

Goblin was far, far weaker than the old man in a fight. If the worst came to pass, sending him back alone would be equivalent to being responsible for his death.

"As long as I'm here, he'll be fine," the old man said. "They'll just wonder if I have some kind of plan up my sleeve. Despite how I may seem, I'm one of the better fighters in our organization. That is, as long as I get to use my ability."

"Hmm? Do you mean to say...?"

"It's not hard to deduce, no? We're an organization of ability wielders. It's only natural we'd have ways of countering them too. My monster fellow there—Rentt, was it? You'd best stay on your guard too."

I thought his warning probably didn't mean much, in light of his misunderstanding of me, but the fact he'd given it at all made a good case for him not being heartless. In fact, he seemed more the caring type, if anything. He just didn't hold back when it came to his enemies.

That was why I said, "Got it. I'll be careful. Thanks for the warning; you didn't have to do that."

The old man looked at me strangely. "And you didn't have to thank me. You're an odd one yourself, you know."

When we met up with Ferrici, she pelted us with a barrage of questions, which was only to be expected. It wasn't too long ago that the surrounding area had experienced a series of massive impacts and explosions. There'd been a giant sticking out of the woods, and a ridiculously powerful lightning strike too. If I didn't know better, I probably would've believed somebody if they'd told me the world was ending. That said, we couldn't exactly give Ferrici all the specifics, but that didn't mean we had to leave her completely clueless either.

"An enemy of ours showed up, and we beat him," I said. "And the lightning was Lorraine's magic. Don't worry. Everything's fine now."

"Really?" Ferrici asked.

Except she hadn't asked me; she'd asked Augurey. She must have had a lot of trust in him.

Augurey smiled. "Yeah. And as for this older gentleman, he's… one of the enemy's allies. We still need to ask him about some things. We're not abusing the elderly, okay?"

Explaining that part was important. We'd look like maniacs who tied up an old man if we didn't.

Ferrici seemed to accept the explanation. Adventurers always had stuff going on that was hard for others to understand, so maybe she thought this was just a part of that. Most villagers were raised with a healthy wariness of adventurers and told to avoid getting close to them so as to not get entangled in their shenanigans. It was a different story for the adults, but it was kind of like being treated as a wild animal.

Ferrici simply responded, "I feel a little bad for him, but I guess you have no choice…"

Surprisingly, after we returned, the innkeeper gave us a warm welcome. I was glad; I'd been convinced we'd arrive only to find our belongings out front and the innkeeper waiting to chase us off. That might have been almost funny, since it would've meant that Siren—who we'd left locked in Lorraine's room—would've been dumped outside too. Then again, Lorraine had given the innkeeper some kind of explanation for her already. She was thorough when it came to that kind of thing.

We hadn't been kicked out of the village or anything though, so I hadn't been that worried about coming back to find all of our things thrown out.

"So, where's Siren?" the old man asked as we entered the inn.

He knew she was in here somewhere, of course, but we hadn't given him the specifics yet. We'd only told him that we'd caught her and restrained her.

"She's this way." Lorraine led us to her room. When she opened the door, we saw Siren, tied up and lying on the bed. She saw us when we entered.

"Mmmf!"

As soon as she did, she began trying to speak, but the gag we'd put in her mouth made her words unintelligible. I could tell that she wasn't happy about the situation though, which probably went without saying. I'd hate it too if I were in her place.

"I suppose we should untie her?" Lorraine asked the old man.

Lorraine probably thought that with all the explaining that we needed to do, leaving the woman tied up would be extremely inconvenient. However, the old man—who I'd thought was the type to care about his allies—took one look at Siren and sighed.

"No, leave her be for a while," he said. "She'll only complain our ears off. Call Goblin over. He'll be quicker on the uptake."

Wow, cold.

Siren, who had been listening, began to get even louder, but everyone ignored her.

"I'll go then," Augurey said. He turned to the old man. "I assume we'll be using this room for our talks?"

"That works," the old man replied. "We do need to fill in Siren too."

Augurey left to go and get Goblin.

"Gramps… What's going on here?"

Goblin, formerly known to us as Yattul, looked both confused and astonished as he entered the room. Augurey came in behind him and shut the door. At the sound of it closing, Goblin jumped a little. His instincts were probably telling him that he'd been trapped and surrounded.

Nevertheless, it seemed the old man had been right about Goblin's ability to keep a cool head, because the tension quickly drained from his shoulders. He showed no signs of getting violent. I could tell that it would be much easier to explain things to him compared to Siren.

"A lot happened," the old man said, "but I'll get to the point. I lost—completely—in a head-on fight. So the job's a bust."

Unexpectedly, the person who looked the most astonished was Siren. Her constant muffled shouts stopped as her mouth slackened and shut completely. Maybe despite her antagonism toward the old man, she'd had a lot of faith in his strength. Goblin looked astonished too, like he couldn't believe what he was hearing.

The old man continued calmly, in a tone that sounded like he was teaching them. "They were real monsters. Few times in my life have I ever met anybody so strong. I used my ability to its fullest and fought without letting my guard down, but I still lost. Can't do anything about it except admit defeat. That's how I truly feel."

In contrast to the old man's gentle words, Goblin sounded flustered. "I don't want to believe it, but if you say so, then… But what does that mean for us?! We failed the job! I know I can't say they'll kill us for sure, but think about who the client is! They'll definitely make us pay *somehow*!"

"Indeed," the old man replied. "That would be troublesome, wouldn't it? But these three made me a proposition. They want to meet the chief, to negotiate. Besides, the organization and our client bear the responsibility for this failure, not us. They didn't provide us with accurate information. If we can make them understand that, then maybe we can all come to a peaceful solution."

"The…chief? But that's…"

Goblin seemed reluctant, but the old man didn't let up.

"I know how you feel. You're thinking that's too big a call for us to make, or that it'd be betraying the organization, but as it stands, we're most likely dead anyway. If worse comes to worst, I could run away alone, but would you and Siren be okay with that? I won't stop you if you are, but…"

He probably didn't actually think he could. If Goblin refused and we couldn't meet with their chief, then we all knew what we'd have to do with the old man. It wasn't like we could let him come back in the future to bite us. I guessed we *did* have the option of letting him go on purpose, but chances were slim we'd have to make that decision, so I put thinking about it on hold for now.

"Of course not," Goblin replied. "I don't want to die either. I owe the organization…but not to the point I'd die for it. I was planning to retire soon anyhow."

"Were you now?" the old man asked. "I was actually going to recommend you do that after this mission."

"So you noticed, huh, gramps?"

"You're a kindhearted man. Unlike me, you're not cut out for this job. It's a lucky thing that all that acting you did as a merchant grew into something more real."

"Yeah. I figured I'd do fine for myself if I kept on with the peddler business. Sounds like it's going to be a long time before I get to achieve that dream though, what with this mess happening."

"Don't say that. Think of it as a chance to turn this into your final job and strive for that instead. You'll feel differently about it that way."

"You say that, but… Bah, whatever. No sense arguing the point. Still, are you serious? About meeting the chief?"

Goblin had directed the last part directly at us. From the look of things, the old man had successfully convinced him.

"We are," Lorraine replied. "We heard all about why you're targeting us, and to be frank, I've had enough of this nonsense already. The thought of your organization sending even more people like *him* against us is enough to make my head spin. I honestly just want to talk to whoever's in charge so I can put all my concerns to rest."

That seemed to strike a chord with Goblin, because the look on his face was sympathetic. "Yeah, gramps is one of the better fighters in our organization. I heard from some of them that he used to be really wild in his younger days. It's…actually kind of ridiculous that you beat him. I'm not doubting you or anything, especially since he admitted it himself. It's just, there's not many people out there who can do that."

"We merely had a streak of lucky breaks," Lorraine said. She turned to Augurey and me. "I never want to try anything like that again. Right?"

"Right," I replied wearily.

"You can say that again," Augurey said, sounding equally as exhausted.

The old man snorted. "That makes all of us then. Don't let them fool you, Goblin. They're more monstrous than I am. Frankly speaking, they're bad folk to have as enemies. The reason I want them to talk to the chief is I don't want to go up against them again. I don't want the organization to either, for its own good. Could you pass that message along to the chief?"

"I kind of expected this," Goblin said. "So I'm going?"

"Who else would it be?" the old man asked. "We'd just kick up a fuss if we all went together."

"Fuss? That doesn't sound so—"

"By 'fuss,' I mean we'll all be rounded up and executed on the spot."

"Oh, right. That kind of fuss. I guess you're right then. But there's a chance that'll still happen to me if I go alone."

"They don't know we've failed yet, so I doubt it. Just trick them into letting us meet with the chief somehow. You'll figure something out."

"You never do sweat the small details, do you? Just like your body."

"Maybe our abilities have an effect on our personalities too, eh? I'm counting on you."

"Yeah, yeah. In for a bronze, in for a gold. I'll get it done somehow."

That was about when Siren began her muffled shouting again. Apparently, she'd finally recovered from the shock of hearing about the old man's defeat. We turned to look at her and paused. I think we'd all almost forgotten she was there.

Then, finally, I said, "Should we untie her? We've kind of finished up already, so it's probably fine, right?"

The old man nodded. "Might as well. But I'm warning you; it's going to be loud. Are you sure you're ready?"

"You think?" Lorraine asked. "I think it'll be fine, personally. Here, I'll do the honors."

She began chanting something that sounded like a spell to release Siren's bindings, which was exactly what happened when she finished. The mouth binding was non-magical though, so Siren removed that herself immediately once her arms and legs were free.

"Hey!" Siren shouted. "Don't I get a say in this?! You think I'm going to sit here and let this happen?!"

"You see what I mean?" the old man commented.

"Don't tell me she wasn't listening," Goblin said.

They both had their hands over their ears as they spoke. It might've made you wonder if they were really allies, but it was probably because they were so close that they reacted the way they did.

Siren hopped off the bed and stepped right up to them. "I *was* listening! Do you really think you're going to pull that off?! Have you forgotten how scary the organization can be?!"

Even so, the old man and Goblin didn't falter; they kept up their defensive stances.

It might have sounded like she was in hysterics, but the things she was saying were pretty reasonable. That said, she wasn't the best at reading the room. We'd kind of reached a tidy conclusion already.

Siren turned to us next. "And you three! Like we could ever agree to—"

She cut herself off and shrunk back when Lorraine stepped forward. While the rest of us were confused by what had just happened, Lorraine brought her wand up to point it at Siren.

"I can do *it* again, if you want," Lorraine said.

I had no idea what she was talking about, but from Siren's reaction, she evidently did.

"Eek! N-No thank you! I've had more than enough of *that* already! I'll be good, okay? I will!"

And then she began sobbing. Augurey, probably feeling as bad for her as I did, approached and gave her his handkerchief. Then, everyone in the room except Siren turned to look at Lorraine. I could tell we were all thinking the same thing: *What did she do to her?*

But we were all too scared to ask.

# Chapter 2:     Departure

"This is goodbye, then. Thank you for everything."

Augurey was standing in front of the wagon, speaking to Ferrici. Behind her was a group of the other villagers, including the innkeeper and the people whom Siren had manipulated. Their gazes were warm.

Since we'd finished collecting all of the materials necessary for our jobs, we were headed back to the capital, and they'd come to see us off. I guess my fears that they'd chase us out had been proven unfounded. Well, that could've been because some of them had spoken up for us to the other villagers—maybe Ferrici's parents or the innkeeper.

Currently present were me, Lorraine, Augurey, and Goblin. The old man and Siren were hiding in the wagon. It was especially important that the latter remained inside, because things would get pretty messy if she showed herself. We were the only ones who knew what she actually looked like, and we hadn't exactly made it public that she was the one behind the brainwashing incident, but this was a small village. Having an unfamiliar face would get you poked and prodded for your identity. That wouldn't necessarily happen to Siren, since she'd pretended to be a traveling performer and had been staying at a villager's home before the incident, but she *would* get questioned about why she was with us.

It went without saying that she'd used her unique ability to trick that villager into letting her stay in their home. I very much didn't want to be there for the aftermath of that particular deception. Yep, it was definitely best for her to stay in the wagon.

As for the old man, I was fairly certain we didn't need to worry about him anymore. That said, we still kept him restrained. Moreover, explaining to everybody we met that we weren't abusing the elderly would get pretty tiring, so that was why he was in the wagon too.

"No, thank *you*," Ferrici said. "You saved us—you don't owe us anything."

"Really, that's not…"Augurey began. "Ah, I suppose it doesn't matter now. If you ever come to the capital, pay us a visit. We'll do our best to help you out."

"I'll make sure to do that," Ferrici replied.

With that, we finished saying our goodbyes and left the village.

Incidentally, the reason we were returning to the capital with Goblin's group was that when we'd asked them where their chief was, they'd told us "everywhere and nowhere."

We'd originally assumed that, after sending Goblin out as our messenger, he'd come back with a meeting location we could then head toward. However, the old man had said, "We have a number of bases of operation, but the chief is most often at our one in the capital, since he needs to coordinate everywhere else. He's probably there right now. But even if he isn't, it'll be faster if we wait for him to come to us, instead of going to him." So that was that—we would go to the capital and then send Goblin to their base there. After that, if a meeting seemed on the cards, we'd go there ourselves.

"Do you think he'll agree to meet us?" Augurey asked. Perhaps because the silence had been boring him, he directed his question at the old man and Siren, who were in the wagon with us.

Goblin was at the reins outside, continuing with his job as our driver. Leaving him free might've seemed a bad idea at first glance, but as it turned out, his ability wasn't anything particularly fearsome. When we'd asked him to explain it in detail, he'd told us that it only let him control and communicate with goblins and hobgoblins. His personal combat ability was actually roughly equivalent to that of an average Silver-class adventurer, but aside from that, nothing was particularly noteworthy about it. In the event that he decided to run, Lorraine could track him no matter where he went. He wouldn't, though, since that would only make him a target in the eyes of his organization.

With that in mind, we'd figured it'd be fine to leave him unrestrained. We'd done the same for Siren too, given that her unique ability and combat strength weren't really concerns for us. To nobody's surprise, the old man was, without a doubt, the scariest of the three.

In a mild tone, the old man answered Augurey's question. "That depends on how well Goblin does his job, but I wouldn't worry too much. He knows his way around a negotiation."

"He does," Augurey agreed. "I suppose that's why we hired him to be our wagon driver in the first place. He has a knack for getting into one's good graces."

"He does. I wouldn't be surprised if it had something to do with his ability. Controlling and communicating with goblins is one thing, but perhaps it works on humans to some degree as well."

Lorraine leaned forward, looking intrigued. "I don't suppose you could elaborate on that?"

"Hmm... I was joking earlier, but unique abilities truly do affect their owners, myself included. For example, you know that I can make my body bigger, but even when I am small, my durability and strength are improved. What about you, Siren?"

"Huh? U-Um... Oh, right! I've always been really popular!"

For a brief moment, a smirk flashed across the old man's face, but he nodded and continued. "If I had to guess, I would say that stems from how her ability allows her to bend the minds of others to make them more amenable to her. It takes careful preparation for her to establish complete control, but even without that, it has a gentle influence on people. It's much the same with Goblin. Unique abilities are indeterminate things and often have unexpected applications."

"Such as?" Lorraine asked.

"One example is that Siren's ability has a slight effect on animals too. Isn't that right?"

"It is. Cats and dogs just *adore* me, but it's not only them. I'd even considered becoming a circus performer because of it."

"That might have been a happier life for you," the old man said. "But there you have it. As for me, I can make the things I'm holding ever so slightly larger. I attempted it with gems once, but it didn't work, so it depends on the item."

Siren's eyes had lit up at the "gems" part, only to fade into disinterest again when she heard it hadn't worked.

"So Goblin's ability might have some effect on people too?" Lorraine asked.

The old man nodded; she'd probably taken the words right out of his mouth. "Indeed. You'd have to ask the man himself... But then again, he might not know. Still, it's not too rare for an ability wielder to notice some kind of nuance about their power like that. Have you felt one?"

The old man had directed that last part at me. I wasn't an ability wielder though. At least, I was pretty sure I wasn't…

There was only one answer I could give him, then. "No, I can't say I have…"

Siren perked up. "What? You're an ability wielder too? I didn't know you were one of us!"

I hadn't taken her to be such a child at heart. On the outside, she looked like the kind of woman who'd twist you around her little finger, but maybe she was actually younger than I'd thought.

Our journey back to the capital was exceedingly smooth. Goblin's group didn't cause any trouble, and hardly any monsters attacked us. Well, the roads we were using didn't see many monsters in the first place. Our outbound journey had just been a mess because of Goblin and his ability.

What's more, the weaker monsters were staying away on instinct because they were intimidated by the old man's aura. And as for the ones that *did* come for us, Siren used some weak mental persuasion to make them pass us by or turn back. These two really were pretty handy to have around.

"Wouldn't you three earn more if you worked as escorts or traveling merchants?" I asked.

The old man smiled. "That's not a bad idea."

"If you can make enough to cover for me too, I'm in!" Siren said.

The old man bonked her on the head with his fist. "Earn your own keep."

I watched her rub her head in pain. The more I saw of this trio, the harder it was to dislike them. There was always the chance this was an intentional strategy of theirs, but that kind of thing was pretty pointless at this stage. Given what they'd done, it was hard to reconcile the fact that I didn't dislike them, but I figured they probably weren't bad people deep down. That didn't mean we could let our guards down around them, though.

And so our wagon continued on its journey. After a night's camp, we reached the capital the next morning.

Our pace had been a little slow because we'd been cautious; we hadn't been sure if the old man's organization already knew about us yet. Fortunately, that didn't seem to be the case. If it had been, then according to the old man, they would've definitely sent assassins after us during our journey. After all, it was more convenient to assassinate adventurers and merchants out on the roads where cleanup was easier, so hits were less common after the target made it into a town.

I had the feeling my knowledge was skewing in a weird direction with this old man and his associates around… But, hey, it was never a bad thing to learn.

I was a little nervous about entering the city. Augurey, Lorraine, and I would get in fine, but I was worried about whether they would let the old man and his group in. We'd removed his full body restraints by this point, of course, but his hands and feet were still bound. Lorraine had done her best to adjust the conjured bindings so they couldn't be seen, but there was no telling how things would play out.

The old man, however, was very cooperative, and we all made it through without much hassle. He and his associates had identification that marked them as merchants. They had several different kinds, apparently, but had chosen those because they drew the least suspicion since they were currently working with Goblin.

In situations like this, an adventurer's identification was the simplest option for getting in and out of cities and villages because it was hard to expose, but according to them, their organization wanted to keep the adventurer's guild from sticking its nose into their affairs.

Even though it made sense that they would act accordingly, I was surprised by their attention to those kinds of details, and also grudgingly respectful of their diligence. They were far from being masterminds though. They could've just registered at the guild normally for legitimate identification. I mean, I managed to, and I was a literal monster.

"I suppose I'm off then," Goblin said. "What will all of you do?"

We'd all disembarked from the wagon except him—he was probably planning on riding it straight to their base. A part of me wanted to go along with him out of curiosity, but that was just *asking* for trouble. For now, it would be wisest to leave things to him.

Augurey answered, "Let's see… Any one of us can do it, but we have to deliver the materials we collected, for a start. That was why we set out in the first place."

He was right. Those jobs had somehow dragged us into a frankly unbelievable situation, but, well, conflict came as part and parcel with the adventuring life. I would've been lying if I'd said it hadn't been kind of fun. Maybe that was wrong of me, but at the end of the day, if a person didn't derive at least a little bit of enjoyment from unexpected thrills or battle, they weren't cut out to be an adventurer.

If you grew tired of those kinds of things, they would eventually sneak up on you while your guard was down and knock you dead. But if you found fun in them, you'd always find it in yourself to be prepared. Something new and interesting could be just around the corner. A life of excited curiosity was as valid a way to live as any other. Then again, the fact that so many adventurers were like that was why most people said to stay away from us.

"Indeed," Lorraine said. "As for these two, it's best if I keep an eye on them. I'm the only one who can maintain the bindings, as well as track them if they escape."

The old man looked a little hurt. "It would be senseless for me to run away *now*. I could hardly use my ability in the middle of the city anyway. And if Siren uses hers, who knows who might notice and detain her. We ability wielders are rather looked down upon in cities, you see."

That sounded rough. He was right though; some pretty formidable adventurers—Gold-classers too—and knights hung around the capital. Sometimes, people even stronger than *that* stayed here temporarily, though it was rare. If the old man used his ability, he'd only be making himself a massive target. No matter how tough he was, I doubted he could shrug off getting mobbed by a crowd of adventurers. As for Siren, her individual combat strength was pretty low. Having control over a few dozen citizens wouldn't mean a thing against a hundred or so adventurers.

Lorraine looked somewhat apologetic as she shook her head. "Even so, that doesn't mean we can simply throw caution to the wind. I still need to watch over you, at least."

"True enough. I can't object to that." The old man then lapsed into silence.

Lorraine turned to Augurey and me. "We should also reconfirm when the grand guildmaster is expected to return. It seemed uncertain, so there's a chance he could come back early. I know the guild staff said it was fine for us to make him wait, but we should still check."

"Right, that almost slipped my mind," I remarked.

"Sounds like a plan," Augurey said. "I doubt he's back yet, but it can't hurt to make sure."

We all nodded to each other, and that was that.

The guild was absolutely packed with people when we entered. There were separate lines for reception, job assignments, jobs reports, new registrations, party applications, and so on, but all of them were long. There were multiples of each too. It just went to show how large a scale the capital's guild operated on. It didn't help that we'd come by during peak hours either.

It was an entirely different world to Maalt's guild. I could see why a decent number of adventurers couldn't handle it and decided to leave. Still, even a place like Maalt wasn't kind to those who underestimated the wilds. Adventurers who did so would only be forced into retirement—or into a grave. The frontier was harsh in its own way.

"No matter how many times I come here, the activity always impresses me," Augurey said.

I nodded. "Maalt's out on the frontier, but it's still a decently sized town. It's not deserted by any stretch of the imagination, but compared to this…"

"Right? I could at least recognize every other adventurer in Maalt, more or less, but here they all blur together."

"I guess that's just how it is. It's kind of sad, in a way, but that's the big city for you."

"Doing your best country bumpkin impression, I see."

We chatted idly, and eventually one of the reception counters for reporting completed jobs opened up.

"Oh, that's our cue, Rentt. Careful not to drop the cage."

By "cage," Augurey meant the one Lorraine had made for us to keep the aqua hatul in. The monster was still inside it, fitted with a special magic tool around its neck that prevented it from creating the water blades it'd fired at us when we'd been trying to capture it. Lorraine had put it on before we departed the village.

Strictly speaking, the guild would have prepared one and placed it on themselves, so we only needed to bring the aqua hatul to them, but the monster was very nimble and prone to running. There was always a demand for them owing to nobles who wanted them as pets, but it was a common story for them to escape during any stage of the delivery process. Since that kind of thing could lead to a cut in the job's reward, Lorraine had taken prior precautions.

If the aqua hatul couldn't use any magic, then even if it escaped its cage, the guild staff could at the very least do something about it. Probably. Since this was the capital, they had a good amount of combat-capable members, but the majority of the staff specialized in administrative work. Still, while catching a monster wasn't easy, they had the resources to manage it.

"Next, please."

Obeying the employee's call, Augurey and I stepped forward.

"How may I help you today?"

"We're here to report three completed requests," Augurey said, handing over copies of the job postings.

In Maalt, the guild knew exactly who had taken which jobs, but the one in the capital dealt with so many people that achieving a similar feat was impossible. Instead, you were given a copy of the job posting when you accepted one, and you would use it to make your report when you finished. The staff could still check who'd taken the job if you didn't have a copy, but that was a waste of everyone's time.

THE UNWANTED UNDEAD ADVENTURER

"Different place, different customs" was a fairly common saying, and it was no less true of adventurer's guilds.

"Let's see, here. Capture of a live aqua hatul, collection of luteum golem mud or clay, and the harvesting of wyvern elata. May I see the requested items?"

"Of course." I nodded and placed the cage on the reception counter. "Here's the aqua hatul."

"Here it is indeed. Oh, but if I'm not mistaken, this isn't a guild-loaned cage, is it? And... My, it's already collared. May I ask...?"

In general, apart from the cheap bottles and other harvesting necessities, which they sold in large volumes, the guild also loaned out expensive equipment for capture requests. It was only practical, since if they didn't, they'd face the problem of adventurers avoiding such requests due to the expenses incurred. Magic tools which could hold monsters weren't cheap, and even if you did have the coin, it wasn't guaranteed that you'd be able to find a place that sold them. Therefore, the guild provided various lending services. That said, they had their own budget to worry about, which was why most of their provided equipment was of fairly average quality, and well-worn at that. It wasn't unheard of for guild equipment to break or fail during a request.

Since these incidents were unavoidable, no blame would be placed on the borrower, but that was only after a lengthy investigation process and lots of questioning to make sure that was what had really happened. Long story short, it was a huge pain in the behind.

That was why we'd decided not to use any loaner equipment for these jobs. The magic cage and collar were both Lorraine's personal creations. While such a thing would usually be a considerable expense, as luck would have it, Lorraine was not only a first-rate mage, but an extremely skilled alchemist too.

Making magic tools was her specialty, and she'd whipped up the cage and collar on a very reasonable budget. The former certainly didn't look like it with all of the engravings etched into it, but according to Lorraine, she'd basically stamped those on and called it a day, so it wasn't as elaborate as it appeared.

"One of our party members is an alchemist," I explained. "She made them. You can just return them to us later."

We obviously weren't going to just hand them over for free. Even the guild's loaner equipment was returned after an aqua hatul was handed over, once the client transferred the monster to their own cage. We just needed the guild to do the same for our equipment.

"An alchemist? I see. Even so, this is especially well-made. The aqua hatul looks quite comfortable."

The aqua hatul was lazily slouching within the cage. Occasionally, it would gingerly touch the bars, only to receive a slight shock that made it give up and lie back down. Every so often, it would try again.

It hadn't been harmed in any real way because of how Lorraine had made the cage. Contrary to what you might think, she was fairly fond of animals. Even if an aqua hatul was a monster, she didn't want to cause it any unnecessary pain.

So why was everything fair game when it came to her experiments, you ask? My answer to that would be...good question.

The female guild employee continued. "Then next, the collection of luteum golem mud or clay."

I began taking the mud we'd collected out of my magic bag. There was so much of it that the countertop began to quickly run out of space.

"Ah. Oh. Um… This is…quite a lot…"

The employee looked somewhat flustered, but the request had never actually specified an amount. It had asked for as much as we could collect, so we'd taken the liberty to do just that.

Being aware of the client's circumstances was a vital part of being an adventurer, but I didn't think we had any problems in that regard either. The client, in this case, was a large—even for the capital—alchemy workshop, and according to Lorraine, they'd welcome as much as we could provide.

She'd also said that luteum golem mud and clay were frequently used in alchemy, and some workshops even made magic ceramics and porcelain items such as pots and jars out of the clay to sell at a profit, so they were always in need of more. She'd been fairly certain that workshops would want to stock up on a lot too, since in about two months, it would be the time of year when nobles threw a lot of parties. For this reason, she'd given us the go-ahead to off-load everything we had, saying she would take whatever was left over. However, she'd been pretty confident that wouldn't happen.

The guild employee, despite her surprise, soon proved Lorraine correct. "As no amount was specified and the client requested as much as we could provide, we will gladly accept all of this."

She called over a few other staff members to help, and they began examining the quality of the mud. When they were done, she turned to us.

"This is all of exceedingly good quality. May I ask where you sourced it from?"

"We got it near Lake Petorama," I explained.

The guild employee nodded, seemingly convinced. "Ah, no wonder. That area is abundant in mana, and the water is quite clean too. The luteum golems that live there tend to make for excellent quality materials. As for your payment, will this suffice?"

The sum written on the sheet of paper she held out was more than enough to satisfy us. Augurey and I nodded to one another, and he signed off on it.

"Finally, we have the wyvern elata. Oh, that explains why you went to Lake Petorama. But...I was under the impression that a number of wyverns are currently nesting there."

"We can't give you the specifics, but we worked our way around them," I said. "The harvesting went fine. Here."

I began taking the bundles of wyvern elata out of my magic bag. We'd pulled them up roots, soil, and all, so we'd wrapped them each in cloth. We had quite a lot of these too, despite the fact that wyvern elata were usually hard to come by.

Sure enough, the guild employee beamed at us. "These are excellent. Few adventurers have brought us such well-preserved harvests recently. I'll take these and see about providing you with a bonus payment."

As a matter of fact, the amount she offered us was an extra fifty percent on top of the usual going rate. Once again, neither Augurey nor I had any objections, so we signed off on it happily.

"That seems to be everything. You've fulfilled all of your requests without any issues. May I have your adventurer licenses for a moment?"

We handed them over, and the guild employee checked them against some documents.

"Oh?" She turned to look at me. "Congratulations, Master Rentt Vivie. Completing these requests has qualified you to take the Silver-class Ascension Exam. Would you like to do so?"

"Wait. Really?" I asked.

Although I'd had a lot on my hands recently, I'd still completed the odd job here and there in my spare time. They'd all been quick ones too—chores, really. Most of them could've been handled by an Iron-class, but since the clients had been concerned that a total novice would only produce shoddy work, they'd dug a little deeper into their pockets and put out requests for a more experienced Bronze-class adventurer. As such, the requests had been counted as Bronze-class upon completion too.

Still, I hadn't qualified for Silver-class no matter how many of those jobs I'd stacked up, so I'd been convinced the day I could take the Ascension Exam was a long way off…

"Yes," the guild employee said. "The requests you turned in today were relatively difficult, in spite of their high necessity, and there was a shortage of people willing to take them, so the merit awarded for them was increased. The requests were also intended for Silver-class adventurers and above, so your Bronze-class status also awarded you a considerable amount of additional merit. As a result, you have acquired the qualifications necessary to undertake the Silver-class Ascension Exam."

"Me…? Silver?"

The news came so suddenly that it dazed me. I *had* known that this would happen eventually. After all, unlike the me of the past, the more effort I put in, the stronger my body grew. I'd fought a string of tough opponents recently too, so I was pretty sure my skills were improving as well.

All things considered, it wasn't particularly weird that this was happening. It was more so the opposite—I'd expected it. Be that as it may, could I have said the same if you'd asked me just a year ago? I had always believed I would become a Mithril-class adventurer one day—my faith in that had been unshakable—but did that mean the cold truth of reality had never once crossed my mind?

No. Of course not. Every time slaying a handful of slimes and skeletons—weak monsters—had brought me to my limit, that reality had hung over me on the trek back home.

The future ahead of me had seemed so dark and heavy. Whenever my mind wandered, the same questions had always ambushed me. *Will tomorrow be the day I die? Is that how it will end for me? Never having achieved a single thing. A corpse in the upper layers of the Water Moon Dungeon.*

Yet now, I was qualified to take the Silver-class Ascension Exam. Was this truly happening? Or was I just dreaming? I couldn't stop myself from doubting that it was real, but Augurey and the guild employee were there, and it was because of them that I knew this couldn't be a dream.

"Not bad, Rentt," Augurey said. "Now we're even again. I must confess, though. I would've liked to make Gold-class first."

"I'm afraid I should remind you that the Silver-class Ascension Exam is *quite* difficult. Although, having taken the Bronze-class exam already, I'm sure you understand that," the guild employee added.

Augurey was openly happy for me, while the guild employee had given me a very pragmatic warning, keeping my feet solidly on the ground. And she was right. It wasn't easy. I'd gotten stronger, but the moment I got carried away with myself, I'd slip and lose my footing. That was exactly right. Still...I was climbing. Little by little, but I was really climbing.

As the joy slowly but steadily warmed my heart, I didn't do a thing to stop it.

That said, I couldn't drop everything and take the exam right away. I had a lot I needed to take care of first. At the very least, I wouldn't be free until I'd negotiated with the organization that had sent Goblin's group after us, and escorted the grand guildmaster to Maalt. There was also the question of the princess, but I could probably put that off for later by making up some kind of excuse. Maybe. And that about summed it up for now, unless something changed.

I'd always dreamed of achieving Silver-class, but now that I was actually qualified to take the exam, there were a number of practical problems I needed to deal with. For one, the prospect of suddenly taking it without any preparation was frankly terrifying. I had to ensure that I was fully prepared first, which included having all the right gear, so taking the exam on the spot was out of the question.

Well, not that it would be *today*, of course. The guild employee had asked me if I wanted to take it, but she'd likely meant the soonest upcoming one.

"I'm happy about qualifying to take the exam, but I'd like to hold off on it for a little longer," I said. "My first time taking the Bronze-class one taught me that it's not something you jump into and expect to pass."

The guild employee smiled and nodded. "A wise decision. A cautious adventurer is a good adventurer. I'm glad to see you possess that quality."

From the slightly relieved look on her face, it wasn't hard to guess that a lot of people signed up for the exam the moment they qualified. Maybe they sourced their confidence from the fact that they'd already passed the Bronze-class exam.

The way *I* saw it, with how nasty the Bronze-class exam already was, the Silver-class one had to be worse. I figured that only made sense, but then again, your average adventurer tended to be the confident type. It was probably more common for one of us to see a Bronze-class exam pass as a sign that Silver-class was guaranteed too. Then, after they'd failed a few times, they'd realize the truth. In that sense, maybe it *was* pretty similar to the Bronze-class exam. At the end of the day, people just didn't like to study.

"I'm not so sure about that," I said. "I don't think I'm that admirable, really. I just take things slow and steady. That's how I've always done things, and it's how I always will."

"You really never change," Augurey said. "You were the same back in Maalt. It doesn't matter what became of you. I'm sure you'll stand firm when you're Silver-class too, and even beyond that."

"I hope you're right…" I replied.

Augurey's comment about "what became of me" had gone unnoticed by the guild employee, but the meaning was obvious to me. He'd been talking about how I hadn't changed even after I turned into a monster. He was right too. My nature had stayed the same. It had when I'd become a monster, and it would when I became a Mithril-class adventurer.

"Oh, are you two from Maalt?" the guild employee asked. "No wonder you're so proficient at harvesting plants."

"Do adventurers from Maalt have a reputation for that?" I asked.

The guild employee nodded. "Yes. They didn't used to, but in the last five or six years, most of the adventurers that have moved from Maalt to the capital have been very skilled. The alchemists and herbalists sing their praises."

"Huh," I said, nodding. "You don't say."

Augurey poked my arm and muttered next to my ear. "She's talking about all the rookies *you* taught. Or don't you remember?"

"Yeah, but it wasn't anything *that* impressive."

I'd only taught them the basics that any adventurer needed to know. Although, since I'd studied to be a herbalist myself, maybe I had been a *little* obsessive about imparting to them the proper way to harvest plants.

"The first surprise every rookie from Maalt gets when they come here is the bonus pay they always earn for the plants they deliver. I know a few of them, and they all say the same thing. Don't make it out like it's not a big deal."

"You think? But anyone can manage it so long as they use a little care."

"Most adventurers wouldn't bother putting in that care."

"Ouch. Can't really argue with that though."

"Right?"

Apparently I'd taught Maalt's rookies something useful. That hadn't stopped the dragon from eating me, though, which just went to show I hadn't been careful enough. I'd let curiosity get the better of me. While Augurey's scares might not have matched mine, I was sure he'd had his fair share of them too. We could both do well by learning from my lessons. We couldn't let ourselves forget how it felt to be complete rookies, taking great care to do each and every job properly. Not now, not ever.

"Now then, I've finished processing your adventurer licenses." The guild employee handed them back to us. "Is there anything else you require today?"

The stock phrase jolted my memory. "Is the grand guildmaster back yet?"

"Do you have business with him?"

"Yeah, I was sent by Maalt's guild to make a report to him about the situation there and to escort him back. We heard he'd be back soon, so I thought I'd check in."

"Ah… I'm terribly sorry, but I'm afraid he hasn't returned yet. On the contrary, we're not quite sure when he even will. We'd truly hate to make you wait too long, so if you'd like, we could arrange matters here to make it so that you can return without him, but…"

If they were willing to go that far, then it was likely they really didn't know when he'd return. Still, that didn't mean we could just nod along and waltz on back to Maalt. Besides, I didn't mind staying in the capital for a bit longer. I was grateful that they were willing to free us from the responsibility and let us go back in the worst-case scenario, but for now, I could still wait.

"No, you don't need to go that far yet," I said. "Just let us know if he comes back. We have some business to take care of here anyway, so it's no problem if we stay for a while. There might be times when we're out, though, so please leave a message at our inn."

I'd been fairly businesslike with my response, but the guild employee looked positively crestfallen.

"Of course… I'm terribly, terribly sorry about our grand guildmaster. I'll be sure to lecture his ear off when he comes back. I can only ask that you please bear with us for a little longer…"

When we returned to the inn, I could hear Lorraine and the old man having a spirited conversation.

"So you mean to say that unique abilities can reside in anybody?"

"By my reckoning, yes. But whether a person can make use of them depends on their individual talent, just like with mana or spirit. All the same, abilities are treated differently…"

"Why do you think that is?"

"It's a historical problem, I'd say. I think, in ages old, before people knew of magic or spirit, there were probably still those born with abilities. How do you think they would've been treated by a society with no special powers at all?"

"They'd likely have been persecuted."

"Mmm. Almost certainly...but maybe not all of them. Some might have been treated as chosen ones, or even as gods."

"And yet, the way ability wielders are treated today..."

"Indeed. But I'm sure you understand why quite well already. Persecution and reverence stem from the same viewpoint. Namely..."

"It's in the name, isn't it?"

"You're as clever as you seem. Yes, 'unique' abilities. Those who wield them are seen as outsiders. Whether they're treated well or poorly doesn't change that. And so..."

"In the present, while the origins of magic and spirit are invisible to the naked eye, the theories behind them are known throughout the world, to a degree. Thus, *unexplainable* powers have fallen by the wayside, so to speak."

"Yes. Unfortunate, isn't it? Consider for a moment: someone with an ability like mine is born next door to you. If nobody around is capable of standing up to them... Well, you'd have a harder time convincing people *not* to be scared."

"This is quite enlightening."

That was pretty much the gist of what I heard before Augurey and I entered the room. Lorraine and the old man, being of the capability they were, had no doubt already noticed us as we approached. Still, that hadn't been enough to distract them from their conversation. It sounded like they wanted to get to the truth behind unique abilities and share it with the world. If there'd been any doubt left in my mind that the old man still felt hostile toward us, it was now put to rest. Maybe, in a sense, he felt like we were all in the same boat.

"Ah, you're back," the old man said. "No trouble handing in your requests?"

The scary thing was, it didn't even feel out of place that he was asking me that. I wondered why. Was it because we were both outsiders in the eyes of society? I was a monster, and he was an ability wielder. Sure, those were technically different things, but if we were found out, we'd be persecuted all the same.

Smiling wryly, I replied, "Yeah. They were pretty happy with how we handled all of them—especially the plant harvesting. They said we were really skilled."

"Really? So that's what you were doing. We never looked into the exact jobs you took."

"Yeah, we were harvesting wyvern elata."

"That's a common ingredient in fever medicine. You dug them up by the roots, yes?"

"You know your stuff. That's exactly what we did."

Siren, sitting at the edge of the room with her arms around her knees, mumbled, "He knows a lot about making medicine. Saved my life with it, when I was little."

"Oho, you remember that?" the old man asked. "I thought you'd completely forgotten, what with the way you've been acting out lately."

"How could I?! I...owe you my life..." Siren readjusted her hold on her knees and buried her face in them, further proving to me that her every gesture was childish.

The old man watched her as he spoke to us, smiling. "She's in her rebellious phase. Despite how she looks, she's still seventeen."

"Seventeen?!" Augurey exclaimed. "I took her to be much older."

Me too. From the whole femme fatale thing she had going on, I would've guessed she was in her late twenties—not because she seemed mature or anything, but because of the bewitching appeal she exuded...or something like that. That said, now that I knew better, I could see that, beneath all the heavy makeup, her features looked pretty young.

"Now you have the truth of it," the old man said. "She's somewhat of a daughter and grandchild to Goblin and me. We'd planned on helping her come into her own as an adult, bit by bit."

"So when you form parties in your organization, you work together for long enough to develop close relationships?" Lorraine asked.

"I suppose we do. Well, it's more like the person with the most seniority—me, in this case—goes around scouting out other ability wielders. The people we choose become our subordinates, forming something of a family, and from there we develop bonds as strong as iron. That's how it goes, more or less."

"I see... So you have allies other than Goblin and Siren?"

"Yes. I just didn't bring anyone else along because I thought the three of us would be enough. But the other...how should I put it, factions? The people who belong to other factions are less known to me. I couldn't tell you much about them."

It sounded like the old man's organization of ability wielders was made up of a number of groups arranged in a pyramid command structure. The person at the top would be their chief, who coordinated them all, so they wouldn't have much reason to interact with each other. They probably shared the same goals and took care to not interfere in one another's work, but it wasn't hard to guess that they weren't close enough to share the specific details of their abilities with each other.

"I'm sure you can guess from what I've told you," the old man said, "but if anyone is going to interfere with your visit, it'll be the other factions. There's a high chance they'll just ignore what I have to say. You'd best stay alert."

Lorraine put a hand to her forehead. "Again with the danger..."

I agreed with her sentiments, but, hey, it wasn't like we had much choice in the matter.

"All we can do is pray that Goblin manages to talk them around," the old man said. "It's entirely possible this will all end peacefully."

I kind of doubted that, considering how my luck usually played out, but I quickly shook those thoughts off. I'd just chalk the bad feeling I had up to my imagination. Yep, just my imagination.

"Oh, right, Lorraine." Augurey looked delighted. "You should hear what happened at the guild earlier."

Even for me, it wasn't hard to guess what he was about to say.

"Did something happen?" Lorraine asked.

"You bet it did!" Augurey replied. "Rentt *finally* qualified to take the Silver-class Ascension Exam!"

"Truly? Congratulations, Rentt! It's been a long time coming. It rankles a bit that you'll be my match...but occasions this happy don't come along often. Shall we have a celebratory drink tonight?"

With how high Lorraine's spirits were, you'd think it had happened to her instead of me.

The old man looked puzzled by Lorraine and Augurey's behavior. "With your capabilities, shouldn't acquiring Silver-class qualifications be easy? Is it really something to be so happy over?"

"The thing is," Lorraine explained, "from your point of view, maybe that's true. But from ours...it's different. Truly."

Her eyes looked a little teary. She gathered herself, though, and prevented any tears from falling, perhaps because her pride wouldn't let them.

The old man inclined his head to the side. "What do you mean? We all saw the strength of the blow he dealt me. For him, a simple Ascension Exam should be..."

From how the conversation was going, he likely had some idea that it'd taken me a long time to finally get to this point, but he had no clue why that was the case. Completely understandable, really.

Nevertheless, we couldn't get into specifics without giving away that I was a monster, so I kept my reply vague. "What can I say? I spent ten years at Copper-class, making a living from hunting slimes and goblins. The whole time, I had my sights set on rising… but I never could. Back then, it felt like I was completely blind to the way forward."

"Even with your strength?" the old man asked.

"Yeah. It was kind of a coincidence, me getting a little stronger. I…never could've seen it coming. Still, now I've finally got a shot at becoming a Silver-class adventurer. I'm beyond thrilled."

"Hmm… A coincidence, eh? I think I see what you mean. So your ability awakened only recently?"

The old man sounded like he'd struck upon an idea. Unfortunately, he was completely wrong. I became a *monster* recently, sure, but it wasn't like I could just say that. After I thought about it for a bit, though, I realized his guess was actually pretty close. It sounded like a useful cover story too, so I decided to go along with it.

"Eh, something like that," I said.

"I see. Well, there's no rhyme or reason as to when abilities decide to awaken. Just as some can use them from birth, others simply wake up to them one day. You're quite a late bloomer, in that regard."

Lorraine spoke up, sounding curious. "When did it happen for you?"

"I've been able to use mine since I was a child. The same goes for Siren and Goblin. If I was pressed, I'd say cases like ours are the majority, but who knows? It's not exactly a studied field, and those whose abilities do awaken late tend to have more tragic stories than we."

"What do you mean?"

"How would you feel if, one day, your friend suddenly turned into a monster?"

Lorraine and Augurey seemed taken aback at the old man's question. I was a little surprised myself—he'd described my exact situation dead-on—but as he continued, I saw where he was going, and I relaxed.

"You see what I'm getting at. It's much the same for when somebody's ability awakens at an older age. Remember our discussion about outsiders being rejected? That practice holds all the more true. A child can…still be loved, as well as pitied, because they were simply born that way. Adults, however… Well, they become unexplainable monsters. That's the only way people *can* see them. And there aren't many folk who'd stay friends with a monster, no?"

Lorraine and Augurey smiled wryly.

"I wouldn't abandon a friend merely because of a change in their appearance," Lorraine said, her tone mild. "So long as they were still the same person inside, that would hold true forever. Although… I might ask them for their cooperation in some of my experiments."

Augurey sounded similarly gentle. "The same goes for me. If standing out from the crowd was enough to break a friendship off, *I'd* be the one in trouble. People see me as quite eccentric, you know. Because of my clothes. But also, because of my clothes."

Both of them finished up with a joke, but I knew they were being entirely serious. I wondered who they were talking about. Just kidding. It was me, of course.

The old man seemed to figure that out too. "You have good friends, Rentt."

"I guess I do, huh?"

My eyes were getting warm, but tears weren't really something my body produced. I could if I wanted to, but it was just as simple to keep them in. It felt like I had a lot more precise control over my body than when I'd been human. That wasn't a bad thing, but it did make me feel kind of lonely. During times like this, it'd be nice if I could just be honest and cry.

"I suppose the reason you can maintain your composure so well despite your ability awakening so late is that you have people like these two around you," the old man said. "But to most of our ilk, the world isn't so kind. Ability wielders are exposed to malice and betrayal…and many end up warped because of it."

"You don't seem like one of them," Lorraine said.

"I shut everybody up with my strength. Besides, I'm older now. It's a surprisingly hard thing to do, keeping a grudge against others burning. And I have something to protect now as well. It's a person's bonds with others that allow them to be human, yes? Even if they happen to be a monster."

The old man obviously had himself, Goblin, and Siren in mind, but his words resonated with me too because I thought he was exactly right. I had people like Lorraine and Augurey who accepted me for who I was. That was why, even though my body was that of a monster, I could still be the same person. I was sure of that.

If the chief of the old man's organization of ability wielders was anything like him, then it couldn't be that bad of a group—for one that took assassination jobs, that is. But, hey, they probably took other kinds too, right?

*Flap flap flap!*

A sound came from outside the window. I looked over and saw that it was a pigeon, and after a more careful inspection, I realized that something was tied to its leg.

"That's the pigeon Goblin uses for messages," the old man said. "You can open the window and let it in, if you'd like."

I figured he'd given us the chance to say no because of the possibility that it could harm us in some way. After all, there was a chance the paper had been engraved with a magic circle that activated a spell the moment it was opened. But although mass-producing something like that would be quite effective for hits, it wasn't very practical, considering all the costs involved.

The most expensive investment would be the pigeon itself. Training one that could fly to an intended destination took time, money, and a whole lot else. And then it would be gone in an instant. Not very efficient at all.

After looking at the pigeon, we turned to Lorraine. With her magic eyes, she could see those kinds of traps.

Paper with magic circles on it was a kind of magic item, and since the spell invariably activated when you opened the paper, it usually came preloaded with mana. That was why it didn't really see usage as a weapon; a trained eye could see through it.

Lorraine studied it cautiously for a bit, then nodded. "It should be fine."

I opened the window and the pigeon flapped over to roost on Siren's head.

She paused, before saying, "Scram, you," but made no attempt to get it off. Maybe she liked animals.

The old man approached her, speaking to us as he did so. "See? I told you animals liked her." He untied the note from the pigeon's foot, opened it, and showed it to us.

Unfortunately, it was all in code, so we had no idea what it said. We asked the old man to decipher it, and as he did so, the conversation kind of drifted toward Siren's ability.

"That was pretty neat," I said. "It flew straight for Siren. Looks kind of fun."

"Sure, one bird is cute," Siren said, looking weary, "but *you* try going somewhere with hundreds of birds with my ability. It'll feel like you're dying."

I pictured it, and it was terrifying. To begin with, birds—especially wild ones—were surprisingly dirty animals. In enough numbers, their droppings would be plopping about everywhere. Gross.

"You didn't have any problems in the woods though," I said. We'd traveled through them just a few days ago, and I hadn't seen any unusual gatherings of birds or animals around her.

"I can keep it in check if I want to," Siren said. "But I haven't always been able to do that. Some of the things I've been through…"

It seemed like she proceeded to put what she'd said into practice right away, because she shifted like she was focusing on some kind of invisible power. The pigeon flew off her head as though it had been freed from a spell and landed on a hatstand in the corner of the room.

Siren exhaled. "Doing that always tires me out." She relaxed, and the pigeon jerked up and flew back over to sit atop her head.

"If it tires you out so soon, then the journey must have been rough," Lorraine said.

"Distance is a factor too," Siren replied. "If they're this close, then I need to stay really focused. But if they're, let's say, outside of this room or farther away, then I don't have to try so hard."

While it sounded like an extremely handy power to have at first, given that it was basically magic that didn't need mana to fuel it, it seemed like it wasn't all upsides. It had its own difficulties too. Unique abilities came hand in hand with hardship in the first place, so it was hard to envy having them at all, really.

The old man looked as though he'd finished reading, so I spoke up. "So what does it say?"

"Goblin met with the chief and managed to reach an agreement," he replied. "I knew it was right to leave the job up to him."

Augurey whistled. "Not bad." It might've seemed casual, but he was just like that. "So where's the meeting place? And are we going now?"

"No, that would be too soon," the old man said. "You're to go to our base of operations tomorrow."

"Are you going to take us there?"

"If you don't mind. But I'm a little hesitant for all of us to go. One of you should stay behind. I'd like Siren to do the same too, if possible."

The old man was, in all likelihood, thinking about how they could be killed for failing their mission if they went. It sounded like he wanted Siren to get out alive, at least. Plus, if we left her with one of us and the organization decided to try and kill the rest of us going to their base, we could threaten to expose them to make them think twice. All in all, the old man's suggestion seemed like the best idea. The only problem was...

"Who's going to stay?" Lorraine asked, looking at me and Augurey.

Augurey quickly replied, "I think it should be me. Oh, but it's not because I'm scared, okay? They could send somebody here after you leave, and since I'm more familiar with the city, I would do a better job of giving them the runaround."

"True, you would," Lorraine said. "Rentt and I don't know the capital that well. Does this work for you, Rentt?"

I nodded.

"Hey," Goblin said, entering the room. "You probably don't need me anymore, but I came back anyway. Got something I should tell you too."

Today was the day we would be heading for the organization's base of operations, with the old man to guide us. There'd been no real need for Goblin to drop by, considering we'd gotten his messenger pigeon, but from the sound of things, they'd sent him to get us anyway. He seemed a little listless, and from his appearance, I could kind of tell why.

"Why are you so beaten up?" I asked.

Goblin was covered in wounds. His clothes were fresh, but they didn't hide all of his injuries. Although none of them seemed too serious, scars and bruises practically covered his whole body. The organization must have found out beforehand that he'd failed his mission, and tortured him terribly.

"Yeah, about that…" Goblin scratched his head. "I explained what happened to everybody—by everybody, I mean just the people gramps personally scouted, not the others—but none of them believed me when I said gramps lost to two Silvers and a Copper. I've got gramps's word that happened though, and I saw that massive spell you fired in the distance, so I doubled down and repeated myself over and over…but no dice. In the end, it turned into a bit of a scuffle, so here I am."

The old man looked exasperated. "Those little… Well, so be it. They'll understand if they hear it from me directly."

He was coming with us to their base today, so I supposed that would all get cleared up. They'd have to believe it if it came from the person himself… Right? I hoped so, anyway.

Goblin seemed to be having the same doubts as I was, because he spoke up, a faraway look in his eyes. "We can only hope… Anyway, I came to tell you all to be careful. You never know with that lot around. Ah, as for the main issue, there's no problem. The chief's happy to meet you."

"How did you get him to agree?" Lorraine asked.

"I said, 'Upon close observation of the targets, we discovered that there were discrepancies in the prior information we were given. Consequently, to our sincerest regret, direct contact became necessary. Furthermore, according to Spriggan's assessment, the targets were individuals who it would be problematic to make enemies of. We were unsure of our chances of success without backup, but left with no choice, we confronted them.'"

Goblin continued. "'Then, our targets expressed to us their desire to meet with our superior. Naturally, this is no simple request, but as we believed there was merit in it, we returned to give our report, to ask how you wish to proceed. Should you wish not to hear them out, then perhaps bringing them back to our base of operations may qualify as us fulfilling our duty?' That's more or less what I tried to get across."

Huh, so he'd decided to mostly stick to the truth? It didn't sound like he'd mentioned that they'd lost to us or that we wanted them to stop targeting us, but those were hard subjects to bring up. I thought that was the correct choice, because if he got too detailed about it, they'd likely just call him a traitor.

Still, given what Goblin had said, there was definitely a chance the organization would try to kill us when we got to their base. I'd manage, somehow or other, but Lorraine would... Actually, she was perfectly capable of protecting herself. At any rate, if push came to shove, we had options. Leaving that aside...

"'Spriggan'?" I asked.

One of the words Goblin had used had me curious. Well, I could tell who it was referring to via context. I only brought it up because I wanted a more definite answer.

"I'm sure you figured it out, but that's me," the old man said. "I'm called 'Spriggan.'"

"Spriggan..." Lorraine repeated. "A type of fairy with the ability to grow bigger. It's said they're similar to dwarves, but not much is specifically known about them. I imagine the code name is derived from your ability."

"Yes. Just like 'Goblin' and 'Siren.' Although I must say, I seldom have to explain it to others like this."

The old man smiled wryly. He was still forced to tell us the truth, so we'd apparently stumbled across something important.

Augurey turned to the old ma—to Spriggan, looking curious. "Do the other members of your organization have similar names?"

"Not everybody, but most of the principal figures, yes."

"Why don't the others?"

"There are a good number of us with weak abilities, or ones that are rather unclear. Finding a name that accurately represents their individuality is difficult. But we only use code names within the organization anyway. We all have our own real ones, of course, so we're not too fussy over code names. You could consider it a form of entertainment."

He was right; the way they picked their code names did sound a little low-effort. If they only used them internally, then keeping things simple made sense. Considering the fact they were supposed to be a secret, us finding out was a bit unfortunate for them.

"Does the chief have one too?" Lorraine asked.

She'd probably figured that if we knew his code name, we could come up with some countermeasures. Curiosity was likely a big part of her reason for asking too. If all she wanted was the countermeasures, she could've just asked about the chief's ability directly.

"The chief is the chief," Goblin said. "The name doesn't represent any kind of ability either."

"What *is* the chief's ability?"

"Naturally, I'd like to say that I can't tell you... Wouldn't that be courageously dashing of me? But the truth is, I'm afraid I really don't know."

# Chapter 3:     The Organization

"This is it."

Guided by Spriggan, our walk through the city had ended with us in front of a building—one that was pretty conspicuous, even by the capital's standards.

Lorraine stared at it, looking astonished. "Are you *sure*? Isn't your organization a gathering of ability wielders with unique powers who take on underworld contract work? You can't expect us to believe that *this* is your base of operations…"

"I understand how you feel, but think about it: who'd ever expect us to be *here*? People don't often pay attention to what's in plain sight. I'd wager it had never crossed either of your minds that a place like this was actually hiding such a shadowy secret."

"Of course it hadn't," Lorraine said. "You were right about it being in plain sight. Landwise, it must be larger than the church or the royal palace."

She was right, though the palace and the church would win out when it came to height. Still, this place definitely took up a larger square area of the city. I wondered which had cost more. Given this building's purpose, its distance from the palace, and its location in the outskirts of the city rather than the center, it was safe to assume that the palace cost the most, followed by the church, followed by this place.

"A colosseum, huh?" I muttered. "Always wanted to visit one, but I never thought it'd happen like this…"

Yep, we were looking at one of the largest buildings in the entire capital, the Vistelya Grand Colosseum.

Several cities in the Kingdom of Yaaran had fighting arenas, but this one stood proud as the largest of them all. It was one of the main attractions of the city. Here, countless mighty warriors and mages had fought countless battles, creating a long history of exhilarating entertainment for Yaaran's citizens.

Tickets—which were tags made of wood—were cheap enough for any common villager to afford, but that didn't mean they were always easy to get. The once-a-year grand tournament, which saw the attendance of fearless competitors from all over Yaaran, was so hard to get tickets for that it was well-known for desperate would-be spectators to be willing to drop tremendous amounts of coin to secure themselves one. The fact that most people wouldn't sell despite that just went to show how popular the tournament was.

Oh, me? Sure, I wanted to see it too, but more than that, I wanted to *participate*. If you wanted to do that, you needed the skill to cut it, obviously, but you also needed to win your way through the preliminaries held across Yaaran. Not everybody had to do that though—some competitors could get in via recommendation. It could be from the adventurer's guild, a noble, a big-name merchant, or even a famous combatant.

It was easy to guess that I never caught the eye of anyone like that. What's more, I hated the idea of paying to see a tournament that I wanted to join but knew I had no chance to. I'd always wanted—and I mean *really* wanted—my first visit to be as a competitor. That said, if *this* was how that first visit was actually going to happen, I should have just swallowed my pride and gone as a spectator.

Becoming a competitor was a pretty far-fetched idea for me these days anyway. Some random competitor hits me with a strange technique, and oh, look, he's a vampire! I'd get people like Nive stalking me, and I very much did not want people like Nive stalking me. One of her was already enough, thank you very much.

"What, you've never signed up as a competitor?" the old man asked in a low voice. "I think you'd make it far with skills like yours... But then, you only awakened your ability recently. I suppose that explains it."

He headed for the entrance, where two people who looked like gatekeepers were standing. At a glance, you might think they were like the guards stationed at the city gates, but their armor didn't bear the crest of the kingdom's knights. In fact, their armor's design was considerably different. I'd assumed the kingdom managed the colosseum, but maybe that wasn't the case after all. Maybe the old man's organization ran it and loaned it out to the kingdom when needed? That would mean the organization had some serious financial pull. It would also make them pretty well integrated into the Kingdom of Yaaran itself.

Perhaps it had been a really bad idea to come here.

Well, I couldn't do anything about it now. I'd just have to grit my teeth and go with the flow. If worse came to worst, we still had Laura. She could handle a trivial thing like the entirety of Yaaran for sure...so long as she wasn't asleep for once.

I was kidding, of course, but the scary thing about Laura was that she made you feel like she *could* do something like that. I doubted she actually would though. She wouldn't have chosen to hole up way out on the frontier otherwise. That said, chances were high that she had a deeper motive for doing that.

The old man approached the two gatekeepers. They looked at him doubtfully, but upon getting a better look at his face, they immediately stood at attention.

"O-Oh! Welcome back, sir!"

We knew from what the old man had told us that he was fairly high up in the ranks. A big part of the reason their chief had bought Goblin's story was likely due to Spriggan's status and reputation. In most other scenarios, this would've ended with their chief saying, "I don't care. Just kill them already." Spriggan must have taken those odds into account when he'd sent Goblin out.

Once again, the old man's cunning impressed me. It was a good thing our interests were currently aligned; he wasn't the kind of enemy we could afford to let our guards down around. Sure, I liked him, and he did have a certain air that made you want to depend on him, but I knew I had to be rational about these things.

"Mmm, good to be back," the old man said. "Is the chief in? I'm here to meet him. Did you get the message?"

"Yes, sir! Vaasa instructed us to let you through down below upon your arrival!"

"Vaasa said that? Hmm. All right. Then that's where I'll go. Oh, these two are with me. I assume that's fine?"

"Of course, sir! Please, head on in!"

The old man beckoned to us to follow, so we did. Surprisingly, the two guards weren't shooting us suspicious looks. In fact, it seemed like they didn't have much interest in us at all. I took that to mean they weren't in the know. They didn't seem to be people Spriggan had scouted, but from the greeting they directed at Goblin with their eyes, they were clearly members of the organization.

"Hey, gramps…" Goblin sounded nervous as we walked.

The old man—*Spriggan* sighed. "I know. The chief won't be below ground."

Lorraine and I looked at him inquisitively. We'd come here to meet their chief, after all.

"The two at the entrance," Spriggan explained. "They mentioned Vaasa."

"That's a member of your organization, right?" I asked. "Doesn't that mean our message got through?"

The old man nodded. "It does. But Vaasa's…one of the people I personally scouted, and…"

"And he's the guy who picked a fight with me the other day," Goblin finished for him.

Lorraine and I both instantly understood the old man and Goblin's concern.

"So you mean to say…" Lorraine said, "he's one of the ones who refuse to believe you lost?"

"Apparently so," the old man said. "Which means…"

"There's a good chance he'll try something?"

"I'm afraid so."

"I don't think we should be heading straight for him then…"

Lorraine was right; it was best we avoid running headfirst into traps as much as possible. Ignore the fact that this was coming from me, the guy who ran headfirst into a trap and ended up with this body to show for it.

"You're correct," the old man said. "But think of it like this: we don't want him making a surprise interruption during our meeting with the chief, yes? I thought it best for our negotiations if we pacified him first. The choice is, however, yours. We are, after all, your captives."

He shook the magical bindings that Lorraine had placed on his arms.

You might think that there wasn't much point in keeping them on since we were already here, but it never hurt to be safe. Even if they only bought us a moment, that was a moment we could use to beat a hasty retreat.

The old man's tone had been slightly joking, but he was right that we had to make a choice. Lorraine and I looked at each other, contemplative.

"What do you think?" she asked.

"I think I've never had anything good come of walking into dangerous places like this."

"Your mistake was strolling into those places to begin with. Not that I get to pass judgment, considering I'm walking into one right now. Regardless, I think he's right."

"Spriggan?"

"Mmm. Meeting with the chief is all well and good, but no matter how smoothly things go, any kind of unfortunate interruption would bring them to a dead halt. Whereas if we deal with it beforehand, we can go in without worrying about it. That sounds preferable to me."

"Yeah… I'm just concerned about whatever it is they're planning to do to us. Do you think we'll end up in a fight?"

I'd directed that last part at the old man.

"Most likely," he said. "Vaasa refuses to believe that I lost, so he'll be raring to pick a fight with you. That's just who he is. On the other hand, that's all there is to him. Trounce him, and he should come around. At least, that's what I do whenever I need to make him listen."

He'd been so casual about it, but that sounded like a pretty terrifying approach to education.

"I'm not like that with everybody," the old man said. Maybe he'd seen the scared look I gave him. "I've never done that to Goblin or Siren."

"Really?" I asked, looking at Goblin.

Goblin nodded. "Really. I may not seem like it, but I'm on the peaceful side when it comes to organization members. As for Siren... her skill set just isn't the offensive type. We know we'd never stand a chance against gramps no matter what we tried, so we never pick fights with him in the first place."

"So this Vaasa's not peaceful, *is* the offensive type, thinks he *does* have a chance at winning, and that's why he picks fights?" Lorraine asked half-jokingly.

I mentally rolled my eyes at her flippant summary, but that was just who she was.

The old man nodded, taking it in stride. "That's him. Though, those traits also make him quite humbled by defeat."

I considered our options, but this was pretty much a foregone conclusion, wasn't it? That didn't mean I wasn't reluctant though. I figured I'd give myself a push.

"If we fought this 'Vaasa,' who do you think would win?" I asked.

"Hmm... I think you'd come out on top, Rentt," the old man replied. "As for Lorraine, I'm not sure. He might be a bad matchup for her."

"Really?" Lorraine asked.

"Mmm. I don't mean to imply that you're weak. Ranged magic is less effective on him. Even if you used the spells you used on me, he'd like as not get back up."

What kind of monster was he?

"It's not that he's as durable as I am," the old man continued. "It's simply that magic is less effective on him. You see people like that from time to time, no? Even without a unique ability to their name. Although, I suppose you could interpret it as an ability in its own right."

Lorraine nodded. "You do. Some people are just more resistant to magic in general. I hear that some are even completely immune, but I've never met anybody like that myself."

"Yes, Vaasa's one of those types. Not completely immune, of course, so enough spellpower will take him down, but anything like what you used on me will also damage the building, so in that sense…"

This was the kingdom's biggest colosseum, so naturally, safety measures were installed all over the place, but it was best to not test those to begin with. That said…

"Magic resistance, huh?" I muttered. "That'd make him a mage's natural enemy."

"Indeed," Lorraine replied. "But that doesn't mean we don't have any options. Besides, resisting magic would also include *healing* magic. Hmm. In which case, I suppose dealing with him first is the best decision after all."

"Why—? Oh, I get it. You're right." It clicked pretty quickly for me what she was getting at.

"If we beat him up," Lorraine said, "he'll stay down."

That certainly made perfect sense to me.

"Incidentally, is 'Vaasa' a code name too?" Lorraine asked.

The old man shook his head. "No. It's his real name."

"Is it now? Then if you had to give him a code name, what would it be?"

"You don't need to ask in such a roundabout way. It's not as if I'll suddenly get indignant about informing on my allies *now*. And besides, you knocking Vaasa around helps us too."

"I suppose my consideration is unnecessary then. I thought if I asked like that, you could perhaps just barely deny selling your allies out if anyone accuses you afterward."

The point Lorraine was getting at had to do with the fact that the organization's internal code names already blatantly described their owners' abilities. With that in mind, there was maybe a gray area where the old man could get away with saying, "No, no, I only told them his name!"

In fact, I was pretty sure the old man was very much capable of leading a conversation to make it sound like he'd given us nothing more than Vaasa's name. And Vaasa himself sounded like a straightforward—or simple, if I was feeling uncharitable—kind of guy.

"I appreciate the consideration, but it's fine," the old man said. "Now, as for Vaasa's ability…"

The old man told us all about Vaasa's ability, including its countermeasures and weaknesses. He was so thorough that I felt as though there could be nothing left, but then again, I couldn't just fully take him at his word. Part of it was because of who he was, but part of it was because when it came to combat, there was a lot that you couldn't understand without doing it for yourself. If you got cocky going into a fight because you had all the information, you'd be tripped up when you least expected it.

As a matter of fact, that was exactly what had happened to the old man's group when they'd tried to deal with us. They couldn't have known that the Bronze-class adventurer they'd been told was the weakest link was actually an inhuman monster who could get back up after taking any kind of hit.

And while it would be terrifying if that actually happened often, there was no denying that the world was, in the end, made up of those kinds of hair-raising coincidences all stacked up on top of each other. I myself was proof of that; I'd never once imagined I would end up with a body like this. Letting your guard down was just asking for trouble.

Lorraine nodded. "Noted. Thank you for the explanation. Did you get all that, Rentt?"

I was the one who would be fighting Vaasa, so it was me who needed the information the most. Naturally, I'd been paying full attention, so I nodded back.

The old man continued. "Apart from Vaasa, other members should be somewhere in this base. I'll tell you about their abilities, especially the one who's likely to pick a fight with you, Lorraine. Goblin, did you tell them that Lorraine hurt me with her magic?"

"I did. I said that while I didn't really understand it or see it, it seemed like a pretty big deal. Actually, what *did* you do?"

"I just cast some ancient spells I studied as a hobby," Lorraine replied. "They came from old manuscripts I found. A lot was missing, but I managed to piece them back together. I plan to eventually collate their methods, compositions, and characteristics into a book to sell to the mage's guild, but as of now, not many mages know about them, which is not to say none. It's just that we tend to be rather secretive about the results of our own research."

That was surprisingly... Actually, it wasn't surprising at all. It was entirely in character for her to go around casting ridiculous spells at the drop of a hat. I thought it was pretty bold of her, but then again, there were more spells than you could shake a stick at in this world. Plenty must have vanished after nobody had inherited them from their creators. Many mages had kept the knowledge to themselves, as Lorraine had mentioned, but sometimes these spells just hadn't been of any use, so nobody had bothered to learn them.

If they were written down, then future generations could use that as a clue for reviving them as Lorraine had done, but I doubted that happened all too often. It seemed that, unless a spell was particularly useful, its fate was to fade away into obscurity, leaving people to wonder whether it had really existed at all.

Lorraine was kind of obsessive about that sort of thing. If she was curious, it didn't matter to her whether it was useful or not—she was the type to begin researching it right away, aiming to use it. Maybe it was lucky that she'd been the one to find those ancient manuscripts.

"Ancient magic…" Goblin said. "Well, it's not like *nobody* uses it. We've got someone who does too, right, gramps?"

"You mean Fuana? I suppose you're right. But was she always the quick-to-rile-up type?"

"Not usually, but when it comes to magic… This one time, I asked her about a poison spell for a job, and she spent the entire night talking my ear off about it. Not that she was angry, per se. When I tried to tell her to drop it, she wouldn't take no for an answer because she said that she wasn't finished and that incomplete knowledge would only hurt me."

Lorraine looked impressed. "Sounds like we'd get along. Although, I'm not sure I could manage an entire night. I'd prefer to establish a proper study plan to stick to, complete with periodic tests to determine whether you'd achieved the required level of understanding, and I'd only let you go if you had."

Goblin gave Lorraine a look that was part amazement, part fear. "You know, I think she *would* get along with Fuana, gramps. Hopefully they don't get into a fight; I kind of *don't* want to see that happen. I mean, I know it'd make things easier for us. It's just… No."

"I understand what you mean, but…hmm, I wonder," the old man said. "Fuana's quite confident when it comes to magic. And besides…"

"Yeah, she's pretty attached to you. I guess a fight is the way this is going to go."

"I guess it is. Lorraine, you'd best prepare yourself. I'll tell you about Fuana's ability too, of course, so do your best. We'll just…sit back and enjoy the show."

I supposed that was easy for the old man to say, since he wouldn't have to fight. Maybe he liked watching that kind of thing in the first place. He'd apparently gone on a rampage in a few fighting arenas in his younger days, after all.

At any rate, we weren't left with much choice. Lorraine and I shared a look, then began ruminating over the old man's information, working out countermeasures in our minds.

We walked through the colosseum and eventually reached our destination. Given that we were underground, the view was unexpected.

"There's an arena down here too?" I muttered.

"We often use this place for sparring," the old man said. "That doesn't mean it's a secret from the outside world, however. You can rent it just as you can the one above."

The exact rental fee for the arena depended on the amount of time you borrowed it for, but it was at the very minimum several hundred gold. I couldn't *not* afford it, but it was by no means easy to put on a show capable of generating enough profit to make it back up.

Well, that was the case for me. Lorraine could manage it. If I had to guess how, I'd say that maybe she could direct a play with her extremely fine control of magic. Mages who could do that weren't exactly rare, but I'd still bet on Lorraine being head and shoulders above any of the ones in the employ of the top theatrical troupes. There weren't many of those in the first place, since most skilled mages preferred to make a regular living slaying monsters and delivering their materials.

Certainly, there were mages in the world capable of finer and more artistic illusions than Lorraine, but they were specialists, the elite of the elite who continuously pursued mastery. None of them would be in a rural nation like Yaaran, and if the situation called for it, Lorraine could switch professions in the blink of an eye and do just fine if she wanted. With a few years of experience and practice, she could even become world-class.

Once again, I was reminded of her ability to make a living anywhere she went. I wondered what I could do. Make shadow puppets with Division, probably. Wow, talk about basic.

"Your members train quite diligently, it seems," Lorraine said.

The old man nodded. "Of course. In this business, losing your edge means losing your life. In a sense, that may make our occupation harsher than being an adventurer. If you fail your jobs, you can still cut and run, whereas we cannot. As our current circumstances tell you, failure or escape only leads us to wonder where the next attempt on our lives will come from."

I could hear from his words how much he meant it too. It made me sympathize with him a bit. I'd never given much thought to the assassination business before, having never had anything to do with it, but the more I did think about it...

It seemed surprisingly not worth it. You'd always be the target of somebody's resentment or suspicion, and you'd never find any peace of mind. The pay was no doubt high accordingly, but even so, it seemed quite a busy occupation. You wouldn't get any time to spend your earnings, instead moving from one job to the next, day after day. If you found another job that suited you better, then of course you would want to quit.

That was exactly the case with Goblin. And from the way Spriggan talked, it sounded like he wanted to retire too, but he had a lot of subordinates to take care of. He couldn't just up and quit. That was life for you: unless you did it perfectly right, climbing the ranks would only land you more responsibilities.

"But enough of that for now." The old man scanned the surroundings. "This is where we were told to come. Somebody should be here..."

The underground arena we were in was level ground surrounded by a ring of spectator seats seven levels high. It was roughly a fourth or a fifth of the size of the one above ground, but because of the amount of vertical space, it didn't really feel confining.

If the organization members sparred and trained here every day, then I could understand why their combat capabilities would be so polished. Needless to say, direct confrontations would be rare because of the nature of their work, but honing their skills was no less important for it. For those who made a living from conflict, strength was always a necessity.

Still, I doubted the old man could gigantify down here—not that he needed it, really, with how strong he was. Just using his ability on his arm or leg would give him enough offensive power to deal a fatal blow.

After we'd been looking around for a short while, a sudden, dazzling light shone into the arena. Actually, that wasn't quite correct. Strictly speaking, it was shining on a circular patch of the third row of spectator seats directly opposite us, deeper into the arena.

Seeing as how it wasn't flickering or swaying, the light obviously wasn't the product of any kind of fire. Even if you used a mirror to reflect it, it would still show movement. Therefore, it had to come from a magic item. The methods to produce tools for magical illumination were well-known, and you could order the end results from pretty much anywhere, but since they were expensive, only public facilities like this one used them.

In ordinary houses, most people still used candles. They could be mass-produced from the fat of monsters or animals. Beeswax and plant wax were options too, but mostly only nobles used them because they were costly. With that in mind, it was clear the organization didn't hurt for coin. It wasn't free to keep magical lights on—they needed to be refilled with mana from magic crystals or a mage, with all the costs associated with that.

To use it so casually... Oh, I should mention that the light was currently shining on two people. One was a man with a large build, and the other was a pretty short...girl, I think?

"You have some nerve coming here, traitors and cowards! I am Vaasa! Strongiron Vaasa!"

"And I'm Fuana the Spellwise!"

After naming themselves, the two leaped from the stands, spun in the air, and landed on the ground. As a credit to their attention to detail, the light followed them the entire way and was even now still shining on them.

"What's their deal?" I asked reflexively.

The old man looked astonished, but in a weary kind of way. "They're idiots. Skilled idiots...but still idiots."

Lorraine looked like she was over it too. "You said they're skilled, but honestly...I can't bring myself to believe you."

"I get it. I really do. But it's the truth. If you underestimate them, you'll be in for a rough time. Stay on your toes."

I sorely wanted to point out that just watching them was rough enough, but he was probably keenly aware of that already, so I held my tongue.

The pair, who had struck funny looking poses a few steps away from us, spoke first, starting with the guy. Strongiron Vaasa, was it? Yeah, him.

"Gramps. Goblin. You have some nerve waltzing right back in here! Especially you, gramps! I'm disappointed in you. I heard from Goblin that you lost a fight. I think I speak for everybody when I say that's a complete lie!"

I'd thought he was disappointed over the loss for a moment, but evidently not.

"With your strength, there's no way you'd lose to a group of Silvers!" Vaasa continued. "Heck, I could eat two Silvers for breakfast! And every time we fight, I'm like a kid to you! Why are you saying you lost?!"

I was beginning to get a pretty good idea of what was going on here.

Goblin was the first to reply. "I told you, didn't I? How many times does it take to get through to you? I was pretty far away at the time, but I could still tell that he got hit by a barrage of huge-scale magic. And he confirmed it himself. He admitted his own loss, loud and clear."

"Lies! All lies!"

Goblin slapped himself on the forehead and turned to us. "This isn't going to work," he said wearily.

Yeah, this avenue of approach was definitely a dead end. The old man took that as his cue to take over the conversation.

"Why do you think I'm lying? What would I gain from doing such a thing?"

That was a straightforward question. He was right too; if he were capable of beating us, or had beaten us, we wouldn't be in this situation. He'd have just killed us, end of story. In other words, the old man was trying to highlight that it would be pointless for him to lie about that. However, that wasn't good enough for Vaasa.

"Don't ask me to read your mind, gramps! You know I'm not good with the specifics like that! I'm not smart enough! But what I *do* know is that you're always thinking hard about complicated stuff to do with our jobs and the other organization members—stuff that's deeper and bigger scale than I could ever imagine! And that led you to this! So there's gotta be a meaning to it!"

"Talk about half-baked reasoning," Goblin mumbled in a low voice. "What do you mean 'stuff'? What stuff? I mean, you're not exactly off the mark, so I guess an idiot's intuition comes in handy sometimes…"

"Hmm," the old man said mildly. "If you're right, then I'm working for the sake of the organization, yes? In which case, there's no reason for you to stand in our way. Why, that's a weight off my shoulders indeed. Now come on Vaasa, take us to the chief, won't you? We can talk on the way there. There's a lot we need to catch up on."

Vaasa looked as though he was going to buy it for a moment. "Oh, yeah, sure. Let's—" Fuana nudged him in the side. "Wait, no, this is all wrong! That's not how this goes!"

"Tsk, thought I had you there." The old man seemed to be replying to Vaasa, but his voice was quiet enough that he was almost talking to himself. "So, what's wrong, exactly?"

Fuana "the Spellwise" apparently decided it was her turn to finally join the conversation. "I see that it's as impossible as ever to let our guards down around you, gramps! But you won't trick us! What's this about a spell hurting you?! Has *my* magic ever brought you down?!"

The old man got a faraway look in his eyes for a moment as he thought back, then nodded his head after finding whatever it was he was looking for. "No. Yours lacks punch."

"Lacks punch?! I can blow a castle wall down! Ha! Unbelievable! You're telling me *you* and your monstrous toughness got done in by a single Silver's magic?! There's just no way!"

I was impressed at how loud she could be with that small body of hers.

Lorraine looked at Fuana with her magic eyes. Even she couldn't perfectly tell how much mana a person had or how good a mage they were, but I supposed she wanted to get all the information she could in advance.

After a short while, Lorraine spoke. "I didn't expect her to have so much mana. She's got about three times as much as you do, Rentt."

Well, that was depressing. I'd thought I'd gotten stronger, but it seemed I still had a long, long way to go.

Maybe Lorraine had sensed my mood, because she smiled wryly. "You're a swordsman, not a mage, and you're thrice-blessed besides. It's not as simple as just comparing who's better."

"But she has three times my mana, right?"

"Well…yes. She'd make the cut as an adventurer and would probably be a first-rate mage too. No wonder we shouldn't underestimate them."

"You think…? I don't see it, myself. They look kind of dumb."

"Sure, but that's got nothing to do with their capabilities. Think about it. Nive's a bit like that as well, isn't she?"

"That's because of the intimidating aura she's always giving off. I wouldn't call it dumb; it's more like you can never tell what she's thinking. It's like looking into a bottomless pit."

"A bottomless pit… I suppose you're right. Nive *is* like that. And I don't get the same feeling from these two."

"Right?"

"Mmm."

Lorraine and I nodded gravely as we observed the dumb-looking pair.

I then brought up the actual main topic. "So, think you've got a shot?"

"Depends on her ability. But yes, I think I do. You?"

"Likewise. Seems like he's the completely physical type, ability included. He probably *is* a good matchup for me."

"Are you okay for weapons? Your sword took a beating in the fight the other day."

"More or less. The shape's still right, so it's not like I can't use it… but I'll go with a reserve sword. It's a cheap one, and I can only pass spirit through it, but that should actually work out better for this."

"That's likely for the best, since he can apparently shrug off long-range magic. Who knows how effective a blade charged with mana would be?"

"Anyway, you're gonna have to use more than words to convince us! Isn't that right, Vaasa?!"

"You got that right, Fuana!"

I could hear their enthusiasm very clearly, which meant that Lorraine could too. It was abundantly evident from the shared despondent look on our faces—not that she could actually see mine—what we were thinking: we weren't going to be able to settle this by talking.

"So what would you prefer?" the old man asked.

The two of them replied without a moment's hesitation.

"Let us fight the ones who beat you!" Fuana demanded. "If they beat us, we'll take you to the chief!"

"If we win, then this is as far as they go!" Vaasa declared. "That goes for you too, gramps and Goblin!"

Well then.

The old man sighed heavily. "Fine, fine. Do as you wish." He turned to us and lowered his voice to a whisper. "There you have it. Good luck, you two."

I wouldn't be surprised if he'd fully expected this to happen. He definitely had a good grasp on the kinds of people they were. That put a sudden thought into my mind.

"Is everybody you scouted such a straightforward idiot?" I asked.

If they were, then I could imagine how rough the old man had it. Goblin was the intelligent type, but Siren seemed closer to these two, albeit calmer in comparison. She'd been willing to hear what we had to say, after all.

The old man shook his head. "Goodness forbid, no. They're just exceptions. Everybody who actually knows what they're doing gets sent out on jobs, so they're usually not around.

These two spend most of their time here because we can only give them straightforward work."

Wow, being kept away from jobs actually sounded kind of fitting for them.

"Which is not to say we don't make them do anything," the old man continued. "There's clerical work, and the organization also has to manage the colosseum. When there's no cloak-and-dagger business happening, we have them handle that. I imagine they have a lot of free time on their hands right now. No tournaments are happening, and nor are any other events planned. The arena has its share of off days too, so…"

"Part of why they're doing this might just be to kill some time," Goblin muttered.

I really didn't want to believe that, but it was pretty obvious from their entrance that they *did* have time to kill. Still, even if we wanted to run from all this, that wasn't an option.

I looked at Lorraine, and we nodded to each other.

"Fine, we'll take you on!" I called out. "Who's fighting who?"

Of course, it was best if I took Vaasa, and Lorraine, Fuana, but we couldn't actually say that; given their contrarian attitudes, there was a decent chance it'd end up the other way around.

If we gave the choice over to them, Fuana, who was interested in magic, would choose Lorraine, and then Vaasa would be left with me. That was the idea, anyway.

To support the plan, the old man added a comment of his own. "Oh, right. Lorraine here was the one who brought me down with her powerful spells, yes, but she didn't knock me out. Rentt here finished me off. With a sword, no less."

No sooner had he finished talking than…

"Then I'll be the one to take you on, Rentt!" Vaasa yelled.

"Hey!" Fuana shouted. "Why do you get to pick first?!"

"Does it matter? Didn't you say you were really interested in the mage? If they're not lying, then she can cast a bunch of spells really fast with more firepower than yours. I doubt that's true, though."

"Mmm... I guess you're right!" Fuana nodded immediately. "Okay, then I'll take you, lady! Got that?"

For somebody called "Spellwise," she didn't seem all that smart. Either way, it was convenient for us to play along. This was all going just as we'd planned, so neither Lorraine nor I raised any objections.

"All right," I said. "That works for us."

We discussed what form the fights would take, and of course, it was decided that we would be using the underground arena.

This arena—and the one above too—was equipped with devices that created shield spells capable of preventing all kinds of attacks, magic or otherwise, from reaching the spectators' seats, so we could fight without having to worry about that.

Since anyone from the organization could operate them, Goblin had volunteered. We needed the old man to keep his eyes on the area so that if push came to shove, he could use his ability to get Vaasa and Fuana to listen to us.

They, on the other hand, knew nothing about this. Fuana was currently sitting in the spectators' seats, looking excited to watch the upcoming match, and Vaasa was right in front of me holding a spear at the ready.

If you hadn't guessed already, he was a spearman. I was wielding a one-handed sword as usual, albeit one that couldn't channel any mana or divinity. However, since mana didn't work on him anyway, it wouldn't be a problem if I couldn't use it. As for my divinity, I wanted to keep it under wraps for now. I couldn't just throw out all my trump cards. I'd done so against the old man, but that was because he'd driven us into a corner.

It wasn't that I was overconfident. Rather, it was because I *wasn't* confident that I was making the effort to hide my tricks. Not that it would matter if it turned out that I'd judged wrong and lost because of it.

"A swordsman, huh?" Vaasa said. "There's no way a needle like that could've knocked gramps out."

He wasn't wrong really; my sword *was* pretty much a needle compared to the old man's giant form. Maybe I could've used it for some decent acupuncture, depending on where I stabbed him. Unfortunately, all I'd actually ended up doing was knocking him out.

"Even needles can hurt if they prick the right spot," I replied. "Want to see for yourself?"

Okay, so it wasn't the wittiest of comebacks, but, hey, this was me. That was what you got.

"Ha!" Vaasa snorted, laughing at me. I didn't let it get to me though.

The old man stood between us in the center of the arena, acting as the adjudicator. "Very well, the match will now begin. Are both of you ready?"

When we were deciding who the adjudicator would be, the answer had been pretty obvious. Lorraine might have been able to do it, but things could get messy if they accused her after the fight of being biased toward me.

You would've thought the old man would fall under similar suspicion for being a traitor, but Vaasa had complete faith in him, saying that he was completely fair when it came to stuff like this.

Upon seeing both Vaasa and I nod, the old man nodded too, raised his hand, then…

"Begin!"

He swung it down, signaling that the mock fight had begun.

First, I figured I had to test the waters a little. I wasn't underestimating him—it was the opposite. The idea of throwing all caution to the wind from the get-go and banking everything on a single make-or-break exchange was just too terrible to consider. At worst, I'd rather fight an endurance match. I hadn't decided whether that was necessary yet, but the decision would make itself clear after my sword had crossed his spear a few times.

Anyway, first swings first. A few steps remained between me and Vaasa, and he was standing with his weapon at the ready. I broke into a dash to close the distance, going as fast as the wind. Figuratively, that is. I wasn't actually that fast. Although, I thought I *was* moving a little quicker than I usually did in combat, but that was because I was using almost all of my mana to strengthen myself physically.

We'd been informed that magic didn't really work on Vaasa, but just because I couldn't use mana to attack him didn't mean I couldn't use it to enhance myself. It just meant there was all the more for me. I wasn't using every last drop, though, because I had to save some in case I needed to throw up a shield spell. While using Division made it look as if I'd taken no damage, it definitely still added up, so the fewer attacks I actually took, the better.

"Mmm?!"

Vaasa looked surprised that I'd closed the distance instantly—fine, maybe not *instantly*, but that had been what I was going for. He hurriedly pulled his spear into a closer guard position and readied himself to slash it at me.

His reaction speed was impressive. I'd been kind of making light of him because of the silly act he'd put on before the fight, but I internally apologized and reevaluated my opinion.

Of course, I still had the initiative. I'd launched my offensive knowing full well he could react. Vaasa made a matter-of-fact, diagonal swing down at me from my left, giving me a feel of his personality. I intentionally moved into its path, intending to twist myself out of the way at the last moment...

Suddenly, I got a bad feeling. In the corner of my vision, I caught a glimpse of Vaasa's mouth: he was smiling. That was when I realized I could sense something coming toward my left flank.

I had to think fast. I avoided the spear, and it continued down toward my right. It didn't *look* like Vaasa was doing anything else, but I had a pretty good idea of why he'd let himself get baited into this situation. It was because of his special ability. I was proven right when I spared a brief glance to my left and saw a number of glinting, daggerlike blades flying at me. They'd started moving the heartbeat after I'd dodged the spear, and they were moving *fast*.

If Vaasa had intentionally been aiming for this opening where I couldn't dodge because my own inertia was pulling me along, then he wasn't as straightforward a guy as I'd thought. No wonder the old man had called him skilled and told us not to underestimate him. With a little more common sense and discretion, Vaasa would make for a great organization agent. I thought it was a shame, and I didn't even care about the organization.

Still, that didn't mean I was going to take his attack. We'd only just begun. Letting him land the first strike would be ceding him the flow of the fight, and I wasn't about to let that happen. Having said that, this wasn't a good time to use Division.

I had to avoid the daggers no matter what. Thankfully, not being human gave me options. The joints all throughout my body had a wider range of movement than would usually be possible for a person. If I wanted to, I could spin my head around—which was terrifying, if I do say so myself.

It wasn't just my joints either. I could bend all kinds of body parts in pretty impressive ways. For example, I could bend backward at a complete right angle. I made full use of that flexibility—er, maybe freakiness was a better term—and twisted my body out of the way of what I now counted as three daggers, which would have hit my head, chest, and stomach.

To sum it up, I contorted my body really, really hard. Enough that if a normal person tried it, their spine would snap into pieces. And my efforts paid off—the daggers continued on their straight flight past me.

For a moment, Vaasa looked flabbergasted at my inhuman movements before he found his voice again. "Wha—? The hell was that?!"

I figured that was fair enough. If *I'd* seen somebody move like this when I was still human, I'd have had the exact same reaction, down to the face and the words. Right now, though, I knew full well that I could do this kind of thing, so it was no big deal.

Vaasa had frozen in shock for a moment, which made him the perfect target. In my new position, the tip of my sword hovered just above the ground, and I swung it up to slash at him.

To give you a better idea of the scene, I was bent over backward, almost doing a bridge, and I'd brought the sword in my right hand into an upward swing. It was an impossible move for a regular human, but for me, it was easy. I had, after all, done extensive testing on how much of this stuff I was capable of. I'd even practiced the kind of scenario I was in now, thinking that a human opponent would have more openings from below.

The issue with it was that, since my stance wasn't solid, I couldn't put much force behind my sword. Nevertheless, I could make up for that by physically enhancing my arms and charging my sword with spirit. All in all, it was an attack that made ample use of my body's unique properties and my own efforts. I doubted anyone had ever been on the receiving end of one quite like it.

"Grrraaahhh!"

At this close range, there was no way Vaasa wouldn't notice my sword coming at him. True to my expectations, he pulled his spear in to defend himself. My sword clashed against it, causing a spray of sparks. Vaasa lost the power struggle and went flying back. That was no surprise; I'd put a lot of power into that attack, and his defense had been rushed.

I considered chasing after him...but then I dismissed the idea. The daggers that had come at me earlier were gone. Vaasa was probably waiting for me to come directly at him so he could use that as his opportunity to strike.

Besides, I could also use the brief lull to fix my stance. I straightened up from the bridge position and returned to my original posture. Vaasa landed quite a distance away and reassumed his stance. I was impressed; his fundamentals were solid. On the other hand, I could see shock in his eyes.

Wait, no, that was terror. Come on, did he really have to look at me like that?

"What kind of ability does he have...? Those...wormlike movements. How...?"

Seated next to Lorraine in the spectator stands of the underground arena, Spriggan had a look of blank amazement on his face. It wasn't hard to guess that Rentt's inhuman movements had been the cause.

Be that as it may, Lorraine was finding it difficult to respond. She knew the answer, of course. It was quite simple: Rentt Faina wasn't human. Therefore, he was capable of inhuman movements. Equation over, proof shown.

Part of her wanted to say it and be done with it, but she knew she couldn't. The old man was being relatively cooperative because he'd mistaken Rentt for an ability wielder. More importantly, the fewer people who knew the truth that Rentt was a monster, the better. A decent amount of people already knew, to be fair, but none of them were the type to let that kind of secret out. The old man seemed similarly trustworthy in that regard, but he also belonged to an enemy organization, so she couldn't tell him.

"I'm not entirely sure myself," she said. "I've looked into it in various ways, but it doesn't seem like something that can be summed up with a few words."

In a sense, that was actually the truth. What kind of monster *was* Rentt? She still wasn't sure. She knew he was some kind of vampire or vampire relation, yes, but that was all. There wasn't enough information to identify him. It wasn't unheard of for, say, a rabbitlike creature to be discovered in the wild and labeled a species of rabbit, wild rabbit, or rabbit relation, but then it actually turned out to be a type of dog.

She truly didn't know what Rentt was. It was almost enough to make her want to get him identified by the God of Appraisal on the spot, but she had too many matters to take care of first. So many, in fact, that she wasn't sure when they'd be done with them all. There was no need to rush, though. Until the answer was clear, she could have plenty of fun studying him in all kinds of ways. She knew it was only a matter of time before they found something, so she didn't feel a sense of urgency.

"Mmm..." the old man muttered. "Fair enough. Simple-to-understand abilities like mine are surprisingly uncommon."

Evidently, he'd found his own rationalization for Rentt's circumstances.

"Is Vaasa's one of those too?" Lorraine asked.

"Hmm. You know how he calls himself 'Strongiron'? It's because he thinks that what he can do is create metal out of nothing."

Did that mean the other members of the organization didn't recognize Vaasa's self-appellation? She found it somewhat difficult to care whether they did or not, considering their code names were more or less a game to them, but it was true that there was no point in having a name if nobody called you by it. Now that she thought about it, the old man and the guards at the entrance had both used "Vaasa."

"Is that not the case?" she asked.

"I'm not completely sure. You see, when he was a child, he could create lumps of salt. He doesn't remember it, but I do. When I had him try it again, he couldn't."

"He lost his ability?"

"The standing theory with ability wielders is that we can't lose them after they've manifested."

"Yet Vaasa..."

"Lost his, yes. Personally, I think it's a conceptual issue. His ability isn't gone; he just unconsciously believes that attacking with metal weapons is the strongest option, so he's found himself unable to do anything else. It's similar to how if a person is convinced deep down that they can't climb up to a high place, they become truly unable to."

"So you're saying that a person's own perception has a strong effect on their ability?"

"I believe so. In Rentt's case… Well, I wonder. When he fought me, his body lost its form entirely. Perhaps he can manipulate its structure entirely at will? Hmm. Maybe I'm onto something with that."

That was actually quite close to the mark. Rentt's Division did exactly that. Lorraine pondered her response. She could refute the old man, but that could instigate a troubling line of questioning. Before she could say anything, though, a shout came up from down in the arena.

Vaasa had come to a stop after being blown back by Rentt and had resumed his stance.

"H-Hey! What was that?! What kind of body do you *have*?!"

Vaasa was looking at me as if I were some kind of creature he'd never seen before. It was a far cry from his high-spirited mood earlier, and though I'd only met him today, it felt as though he wasn't acting like himself.

"What kind?" I replied. "This kind."

I spun a number of various joints around to show him, including my neck, which I turned so my head was facing backward.

Hmm. It was strange seeing things from this point of view, if I did say so myself, but this didn't mean I was letting my guard down; I still had my senses focused behind me.

With a series of cracking noises, I returned my head to its original position and saw that Vaasa looked even more terrified than before. Seriously? After all the trouble I went to, giving him a detailed demonstration... Just kidding. Of course he'd react that way.

"What are you? A monster?!"

"That's a bit much, coming from somebody who's colleagues with that old giant. I'd say he ranks way above me when it comes to monster impressions."

"I mean, yeah, but you're pretty up there yourself."

Oh, he agreed with me. I didn't think he'd treat his coworker as a monster like that. However, that didn't mean I could agree with *him*. I was human. Well, that was actually a work in progress, but still.

"No, I'm totally normal," I said. "Anyway, you're not one to be pointing fingers. What was with those daggers earlier? They appeared out of thin air and disappeared just as fast."

I knew why they had, but it was worth asking all the same. I didn't think the old man had lied to me—it was just that Vaasa might let some new information slip. Who better to ask than the person himself?

"My ability is pretty normal," Vaasa said. "I call it 'Strongiron.' I can create and vanish metal in any shape, whenever and wherever I want."

"So you could create gold and sell it?"

Now that was an exciting prospect. Given Vaasa's reaction, though, he might have thought that I was making fun of him.

"As if! Uh... Well, that's not actually *impossible* for me, but I can't make that much gold anyway. Besides, whenever I release my ability, the metal I create disappears."

In which case, he probably had limits on the amount of other kinds of metal he could create too. Maybe that was why he'd only created three daggers earlier? His own concentration could be a factor too. But just as I thought, his ability wasn't limitless.

The old man had possessed an unlimited well of endurance and stamina, but that could have all come from training. Plus, Goblin had mentioned that constant usage of his ability had gradually let him control more goblins at once. It seemed that no matter what form your power took, you had to train if you wanted to become strong.

Now then, I had a pretty good grasp on Vaasa's ability. Like me, he could still have tricks up his sleeve, but if I let that stop me from going on the offensive, this fight would never go anywhere. Combat always came with risks. Victory went to those who went in knowing that. Or so my theory went.

"All right, let's pick this back up," I said. "Here I come."

I hadn't *needed* to say that, but Vaasa was giving off the impression that he was kind of out of it after the shocks he'd received. While I could have kept that advantage and attacked him, I didn't want him crying foul because of it after the fight. I would win this fight fair and square. That is, if you could call having a body that could take fatal injuries and recover to be as good as new "fair."

Vaasa grunted. "Bring it on!"

My words had shaken him out of his half-daze, and he schooled his expression back into seriousness as he gripped his spear. His stance was tight; I couldn't see any openings. I couldn't tell exactly how much he'd recovered, but it was clear that he wasn't letting my potential monstrousness get to him anymore.

Once I confirmed that, I charged him once more. This time, I made use of proper swordsmanship to slash at him. Catching a human enemy off guard with inhuman movements was all well and good, but from a power perspective, forced, unnatural movements could only be about seventy percent as effective as the real deal. The only reason I could even use them was because I used spirit and mana to brute force the issue. In a proper fight, the swordsmanship that I'd been refining since the start of my adventuring career was far more comfortable to use.

Perhaps it had been too easy to read, however, because Vaasa deflected my sword with his spear. He then continued the movement, bringing his spear down and aiming a thrust at my chest, which was completely undefended. That didn't matter, though, because I bent over backward and dodged his strike.

"Again?!" Vaasa cried.

It wasn't the first time he'd seen it, but I didn't blame him for not adapting. Who'd ever expect their opponent to do that in a fight?

Vaasa hesitated for a moment, perhaps because he didn't know what to do with his spear next. I followed through with my movement and placed my hands on the ground behind me, using the momentum to do a handstand and kick his motionless spear as hard as I could just below the tip on my way up. I didn't stop there though; I sprung off my hands into a backflip and my feet landed back on the ground, which I kicked off of as I went for Vaasa.

This had all happened in a single moment, so he hadn't brought his spear back down into a neutral stance yet. Right now, he could see me and read my next move, but he had no way of stopping me. I stepped in close to him and brought the sword I'd been holding behind me around in a horizontal slash at his chest.

All it resulted in was a loud, high-pitched *clang*. I looked closer and saw something that looked like a sheet of metal covering Vaasa's chest. It was obvious that it hadn't been there earlier, because he was wearing light leather armor.

That meant it had to have been created by his ability. As if to prove that, the very next moment, it shifted shape into a number of arrow-like projectiles which shot straight at me. They were a lot smaller than the daggers from earlier, but because of the sheer amount of them, they would be hard to avoid.

I couldn't dodge straight back because I was so close, so I zigzagged as I retreated instead. Nonetheless, I couldn't manage to avoid them completely, and one grazed my shoulder. My robe was in the way though, and its ever-reliable defensive capabilities rarely let anything through. The tiny arrow deflected off of it.

Vaasa, perhaps motivated by seeing my retreat, came for me. His spear offensive was fierce. It began with a vertical slash, which immediately turned into a sweeping, horizontal cut after I dodged it, which *then* turned into a thrust after I jumped back.

My sword was lowered, and I wouldn't be able to bring it up in time to block. He'd put a spin on his spear thrust, so if it hit me, it would pierce deep. I definitely didn't want that to happen, but when I made to dodge, more metal arrows appeared in my way and shot toward me.

Vaasa's ability was a huge pain to deal with. I was forced to admit that in circumstances like these, it was worth its weight in gold.

Arrows or spear? Either way, I'd get stabbed, damn it. Still, the arrows were the obvious choice—they had less power behind them. Left with no other alternatives, I headed straight toward them. It was the only way I could get away from his spear.

"Hmm?!"

Getting pierced by a few arrows wasn't a huge deal to me because of my body, but apparently Vaasa hadn't been expecting my movement. He looked surprised, but not as much as last time—his spear didn't stop.

That was a shame, actually, since it might have given me an opening to get clear. Anyhow, just as I'd expected, I plunged into the spray of metal arrows created by Vaasa's ability, and they pierced the left side of my body. However, because they'd just manifested, there hadn't been as much force behind them as I'd thought, so I got away with only shallow wounds.

I thanked my good fortune, and with the brief respite I'd created for myself, I brought my sword back up, charged it with spirit, and swung it at the head of Vaasa's spear.

He'd gotten in close and cornered me with his offensive, but this was also my biggest opportunity. What's more, since his arrows were still stuck inside me, it was hard to imagine that he could use his ability for defense. My read on him so far told me that he couldn't create more metal until he'd retrieved what he'd already made. There was a chance he was only pretending, but right now, that was easily a bet I was willing to take.

And it paid off. My spirit-charged sword connected just below the tip of his spear and cut through, sending it flying away.

"Aw, crap!" Vaasa yelled.

He interrupted his offensive and fell back, probably because he'd judged that continuing with a close-range fight wouldn't be wise.

Payback successful. I looked over at Vaasa, a small part of me hoping that breaking his weapon meant that I'd won, but he still looked raring to go. The fight was still on…

I wondered how Vaasa was planning to fight me now. As I watched him, I saw him visibly begin to concentrate on something. Then metal started forming at the tip of his broken spear, creating a new spearhead.

Ah. Maybe I should have expected that, given his ability. Even so, how durable and strong would it be? It seemed kind of like a rushed patch job. Then again, there was only one way to find out. Before Vaasa could completely finish his preparations, I dashed straight for him.

"Hmph!" Vaasa didn't look like he'd expected me to wait; he reacted right away. He blocked my downward cut with the shaft of his spear, between where he was gripping it. Up close, I saw that the grip had a thin metal coating—one that felt strongly reinforced.

His ability truly was extremely versatile. If he put more thought into it and polished it, he could become pretty fearsome, but as it was, it looked like I was still more than a match for him.

Maybe the old man had high expectations for Vaasa too. If he made him fight a myriad of enemies for more experience, then— Hey, wait. Was *I* one of those enemies? I wouldn't put it past the old man to have set things up so his side could benefit a little too.

Vaasa's movements were a little different now. It wasn't that they had dulled; they had just changed. Before, he'd thrust and struck at me like any other spearman would have, but now he was moving more like a staff wielder. He'd probably trained as both so that he could keep fighting even if his speartip broke. It made perfect sense, considering that he could reform his speartip with his ability during a fight and shift back into being a spearman.

Given his occupation, I figured that he didn't always need to kill his targets. Sometimes, he needed to bring them in alive. It sounded entirely plausible for the organization to commit kidnapping and extortion. In such cases, stabbing a hole in the victim and killing them would be problematic. A staff gave him the benefit of restraint, and he could use it to beat them up, knock them out, that kind of thing.

Vaasa's staff moved like it was dancing as he parried my attacks, while my sword stabbed and slashed at him at inhuman angles and timings that prevented him from stringing together a moment of focus. It seemed he had gotten used to the freakiness and unpredictability of my body, but adjusting long-established, ingrained habits in one's movements wasn't something that you could do on the fly. Spearmanship established under the premise that your opponent had the range of motion of a normal human wouldn't deal with my movements well.

When it came to the first-rate masters, my trickiness obviously wouldn't pose much of a problem. There were people out there like Nive, who moved so smoothly that she could deal with Division-using vampires.

It was a different world, up at her level, but Vaasa wasn't there. Gradually, my attacks started connecting. His stamina was running out. Continuously dealing with unusual movements and thrusts from unexpected directions wasn't just a drain on your physical endurance; it was a drain on your mental endurance too.

In contrast, the concept of stamina barely existed for me in the first place, and my mental fortitude was a lot more steadfast compared to back when I'd been human. If I felt like it, I could fight for three or four days straight. Winning a contest of endurance against an undead opponent was an uphill battle. And that wasn't even the full extent; I could shrug off dozens of fatal wounds as if they were nothing. I understood why undead had been so feared back in ancient times.

"Damn it!" Vaasa muttered, glaring at me. He probably understood that his situation was only getting worse. He gripped his spear tight. Its tip had already finished reforming, and he was moving like a spearman again.

"It's time I finished this," I said.

"Not if I can help it!" He readied his spear and thrust it at me.

Compared to him, who was covered in wounds, I was basically unharmed. Strictly speaking, we'd injured each other a roughly equal amount; I'd just taken blows instead of cuts. However, my undead body had been quick to mend them each time, so outwardly, I was completely unscathed. Sure, there was a limit on the amount of life force I could draw from, but the fact that my body would be in perfect condition until that ran out was pretty unfair.

It wasn't my fault that it worked that way, so cut me some slack. Still, I did feel a little bad that none of this felt "fair and square."

Vaasa's thrust came straight at me, but it was weak. I figured it would be easy to dodge, but the moment I thought that...

"Take this!" Vaasa shouted, and his spear tip flew at me like an arrow.

Ah. He could do that because he'd created the tip with his ability. While he hadn't caught me off guard, the projectile was flying a little harder and faster than I'd expected. Maybe being driven into a corner had given him a burst of strength, or maybe he'd set things up so that he could bet everything on this moment. I didn't know. But his spear tip flew straight and, before I could get out of the way, stabbed into my stomach.

"Yes!" With newfound momentum, Vaasa stepped in to follow up on his attack. That was natural; usually, it would be the kind of wound that dulled a person's reactions no matter how hard they tried to fight on. However...

"That kind of stings." With the spear tip still in my stomach, I ignored it as I moved in toward Vaasa, my movements no different to how they'd been earlier.

"Wh-What?!"

Naturally, my lack of reaction flustered him, which only made sense. No human could take an arrow to the stomach and maintain the exact same look on their face, much less move about unimpeded, but I wasn't human, and that was that. If I *had* been human, I probably wouldn't have won, for starters.

As I pondered that, I brought my sword down on his head. I wasn't going to kill him, of course, so I used the flat of the blade. My aim was true, and I scored a direct hit.

"Ack!"

Vaasa immediately collapsed. His eyes rolled back up into his head, and he lay there unmoving.

"Hey, you're alive...right?" A little worried that I'd put too much into my swing, I approached and checked on him.

After I confirmed that he was indeed alive, I looked at the old man.

"He's completely knocked out. It's your win, Rentt."

"Wh-What was *that*?!" yelled a voice to Lorraine's side, from the spectators' stands. The old man had already descended to check if Vaasa was out cold.

Though he'd been the adjudicator for the fight, announcing the start and preventing outside interference was all that had been necessary of him, so there had been no issue with him sitting in the stands. He'd had to get up close to check if Vaasa was still alive or just unconscious, but that was a given.

Lorraine looked toward where the yell had come from and saw Fuana the Spellwise. She was finding it hard to believe the fight she'd just watched. Her disbelief likely didn't stem from Vaasa's defeat and her sense of camaraderie and faith in him, but simply from Rentt's movements.

Lorraine had been with Rentt the longest, ever since he'd obtained his undead body, and even she still found it difficult to believe on occasion. It was easy to imagine how much of a shock it would be to someone seeing it for the first time.

Sensing a chance to have some fun, Lorraine called out to Fuana. "Is something wrong?"

"'Is something wrong?' Of course there is! Didn't you see that?!"

"See what?"

"He moved like he doesn't have a spine! Vaasa landed a decent amount of hits, but he didn't react at all! Not even at the end when that spear tip stabbed into his stomach!"

Undead did, in fact, have spines, but their bodies were as pliable as mollusks. It was a unique characteristic of theirs that almost any kind of damage done to them was meaningless up until the point their existence could no longer hold itself together and snuffed out. That was why Rentt hadn't reacted to Vaasa's hits, or even the spear tip. However, she couldn't explain that, and even if she could, there was no guarantee Fuana would buy any of it. Left with no alternative, Lorraine chose to give what could perhaps be considered a slightly inaccurate excuse.

"That's just his ability, no? When I saw Vaasa use his— it's called Strongiron, right?—I felt the same way. An ability that creates weapons out of thin air? I wanted to yell at him to be more considerate of the laws of physics."

Truth be told, she *was* wondering how Vaasa did it. She could understand magic and spirit techniques, because they were phenomena that manifested using the energies of mana and spirit respectively. All the same, she had the impression that unique abilities were derived from something else. They didn't appear to use any kind of energy. Perhaps, like with mana, only those who possessed it could feel it, but...

In that sense, both Rentt and Vaasa seemed equally unusual to a "normal" human like her.

Despite being an ability wielder herself, Fuana clearly still found Rentt strange. "Even gramps would show *some* kind of reaction after taking that many hits! That ability is just... It's just weird!"

"You think?" Lorraine said. "I wonder if there's a limit on the range of possible abilities. I don't really have a sense for that myself though…"

Before their oddly mismatched conversation could continue…

"Whew, managed to get the win."

Rentt approached the spectator stands. Beside him was the old man, who was carrying Vaasa over his shoulder—very easily too, which almost felt odd given the unconscious man's large frame, but given the old man's true nature, it made complete sense. If he wanted to, he could grow to become several times larger than Vaasa.

The old man reached the stands and casually tossed Vaasa into them.

"Whoa, hey," Rentt said worriedly. "Will he be okay? I just knocked him out. Shouldn't you be a little more careful with him…?"

The old man snorted. "He doesn't train the way he does so that something like that would be enough to harm him. Besides, he let his guard down far too much. A little rough treatment won't hurt him."

"I thought he put up a good fight, personally. Especially considering I was his opponent."

"Hmm? Is that dissatisfaction I spy on your face?"

"No, it's not like that… I just figured I was a little unfair."

Rentt was probably talking about how he'd essentially brute-forced the win by virtue of being undead. Even if his level of ability was equal, or even a rung lower, inexhaustible stamina and endurance could give him the win eventually anyway. In essence, perhaps he felt that he hadn't won on his own merit.

However, the old man replied, "Even if you forced the win with your ability, that still counts as your own skill. In the first place, consider this: we're an underworld organization that tried to assassinate you. He challenged you to a direct fight without doing any research beforehand and lost. It's obvious which of you is the fool."

The old man's tone sounded derisive of himself, likely because he'd made the same mistake just a few days ago. Still, even then, he, Goblin, and Siren had received information from the organization, done their best to avoid notice, and only resorted to the brute-force approach after everything else had failed. By comparison, Vaasa had chosen to charge in headfirst, which only further supported the old man's reasoning.

"You think?" Rentt asked.

"Yes. In that sense, this was his complete defeat. You diligently acquired information on him from me and challenged him after planning reasonable countermeasures. Hopefully, he comes away from this having learned his lesson in that regard..."

"I knew it. You *were* using me to teach him."

"Ho? So you noticed? It's fine, no? This way, nobody loses out."

"That's only assuming your organization doesn't put a target on our backs again..."

They'd come here to prevent that, but there was no telling what would happen.

"I certainly hope not," the old man said. "I've had enough of you lot already. Don't worry. I'd refuse the order if it was given."

"Mmm, well...let's leave it at that for now, I guess." Rentt turned to Lorraine and Fuana. "So, you two are up next, right? Are you ready?"

"Yes, I can start whenever," Lorraine replied.

"Huh?!" Fuana exclaimed. "Uh, I-I, um, yeah, I'm *always* ready!"

Her voice sounded oddly shaky. Evidently, Rentt's match had been quite a shock to her.

In the underground arena, two women stood facing each other. One was an adult who exuded the aura of a profoundly wise mage, while the other had the appearance and height of a young girl and was clad in robes that looked a little too big for her body.

The adult was Lorraine, the girl was Fuana the Spellwise, and their fight was about to begin. Like my fight with Vaasa, the adjudicator was the old man—Spriggan.

Like earlier, he wouldn't enter the arena during the fight. He would be carrying out his role from the spectators' stands, just before the mana barrier. You might think he should watch from closer up, but given the scale of our fights and the ranges of our attacks, he had to be where he was.

A fight like mine and Vaasa's, where we mainly used a sword and spear, was one thing, but area attacks were the bread and butter of a fight between mages. If he was in the arena, it wouldn't matter how careful he was—there was always a chance he'd get hit by stray projectiles from bombardment spells. Therefore, he had to adjudicate from outside. He was skilled and tough enough to endure being inside, but it was silly to expect him to carry out his role while being bruised and battered.

As such, this was the most logical option; not only for fights between mages, but for fights between ability wielders too, because they often played out similarly. If two people with an ability like the old man's clashed, the resulting small arena would leave nowhere to run. What a terrifying thought.

"Very well, the match will now begin. Are both of you ready?"

In a voice that didn't match his small frame, the old man's question boomed throughout the entire arena. The two fighters nodded.

"Then…begin!"

Fuana was the first to make a move. At the old man's signal, she focused her mana, then fired an unchanted Fotiá Volídas, a fireball. The fact that it was several times the size of a regular mage's, coupled with how fast she'd manifested it, made it clear that she was skilled.

Fotiá Volídas wasn't a particularly advanced spell, so being able to use it wasn't anything to brag about, but neither was it anything to make light of. It maybe wouldn't hurt a tough monster, but a direct hit would definitely ruin a regular human opponent's day. It was quick to manifest and didn't consume much mana. Plus, like with the one Fuana had just fired, you could adjust its strength and size. That wasn't all though.

Once Lorraine saw that Fuana had fired a Fotiá Volídas, she began moving to the right to get out of its way. Naturally, she'd enhanced her physical abilities with mana, so she could move far faster than your average person. In addition, although she was a mage, she knew her way around non-magical combat too, so her movements were practiced and smooth.

Back when she'd first arrived at Maalt, all she'd had was her skill as a mage. She hadn't been able to handle trips into the forest or fights with monsters at all, but she'd spent the last ten years diligently training and learning. She was lightning quick on the uptake at pretty much any subject to begin with, and a hard worker on top, as well as extremely intelligent—way more than a guy like me. Before I knew it, she'd learned how to move quite smoothly, with an agility you wouldn't expect from a mage.

I was happy to see her growth, because I'd been watching her since way back. That said, at the end of the day, she was a mage, so it was rare for her to go into a fight with a sword in her hand.

For this fight, all she was holding was a single, small wand. She could cast magic just fine without it, but when it came to mana expenditure, firing speed, and the like, it made a difference. Not only that, but she'd also told me that she could use it to feint attacks against her opponent. After all, since most mages fired spells from the tips of their wands, her opponent would unconsciously focus on it, despite the fact that Lorraine could fire a spell from anywhere she wished. If the tip of her wand was all they were thinking about and her spell suddenly came from directly below, they'd be in for a shock.

I was getting off topic, wasn't I?

Lorraine dodged Fuana's Fotiá Volídas, but the fireball suddenly veered off from its direct course at a right angle and began pursuing her.

This was the strength of the relatively simple-to-cast Fotiá Volídas. After you fired it, you could easily manipulate its flight path. You could do this with other spells too, but the more advanced you got, the harder it was to do.

In that sense, Fotiá Volídas was easy to handle. Needless to say, Lorraine would be prepared for that. She smiled at the pursuing fireball, then ran directly toward Fuana. Right before she reached her, she pulled a dagger from her waist and aimed it at Fuana's neck. You didn't see her doing it often, but this was in Lorraine's repertoire too. Then, the barest moment before the fireball hit her back, she dodged to the left.

The fireball, unable to pursue her, continued straight toward Fuana. Lorraine had been too fast—even more so than earlier. She must have increased the amount of mana she was using to physically enhance herself at that moment.

Just when I thought the fireball would hit Fuana head-on, she stretched her hand out toward it and let out a shout.

"Haah!"

It was suicidal. It went without saying, but magic wasn't so convenient that your own spells wouldn't harm you. What *should* have happened was Fuana's arm exploding into flames, but instead, the fireball suddenly vanished, leaving only an unharmed Fuana standing there. While that had been going on, Lorraine had backed off, and the two were now facing each other at a distance similar to the start of the fight.

"Is that her 'Spellwise' ability?" I asked the old man, who was nearby.

He nodded. "'Spellwise' is just what she calls herself, but yes. Like I told you earlier, it lets her see the weakest part in the structure of a completed spell. You might be tempted to think of it similarly to magic eyes, but while those allow a person to perceive things such as the flow or amount of mana, Fuana's ability is fundamentally different. Hmm, how should I explain this? To use the body as an example, if a person's magic eyes can see the places where blood gathers and allows them to estimate where the heart and brain are, then Fuana just knows where the heart and brain are at a glance."

"I'm not sure I get it. The person with magic eyes would know where the heart and brain are too, right? Based on the locations where blood gathers."

"Yes, but they would have to go through the process of reasoning to realize that. Fuana knows it intuitively, in an instant. She doesn't have to think; that's just how it is for her. Keep watching, and you'll see what I mean."

So she could see the weakest point in a spell at a glance. That seemed like a strong ability—enough to make her a natural enemy of any mage. It was equal to Vaasa's resistance to magic.

"Fuana must be a bad matchup for Lorraine then too, huh?" I said.

The old man tilted his head slightly. "Not necessarily. Vaasa nullifies magic without doing anything, but that isn't the case for Fuana. Look."

I did as he said and saw that Lorraine was circling Fuana at a run, looking amused and firing spells at regular intervals. Vráchos Volídas, Hydor Volídas, Anemos Volídas—using the most fundamental of spells of each element, Lorraine cast projectiles of earth, water, and wind one after another.

Nonetheless, Fuana brought her hand up and, with a burst of mana, erased every single one before they touched her. When she'd done that to the Fotiá Volídas earlier, it had looked like she'd touched the fireball, but strictly speaking, she'd just unleashed mana from her palm to disrupt the structure of the spell before it hit her.

Now *that* was useful. But while I'd have loved to learn that trick for myself, I wasn't capable of determining a spell's weak point at a glance. Spell structures weren't fixed, so their weak points were always moving. I could see that even when the spells coming at her were the same ones, Fuana would reach her palm out to slightly different spots each time. In short, it was a feat that you could only pull off if you had her unique ability.

I figured even Lorraine would have trouble dealing with it, but when I looked over at her expression, it was still perfectly at ease. In fact, she looked like she was having fun. It wasn't the face she made when she'd landed in a sticky situation, but the one she made when she'd found something that caught her interest. Whether it was with her experiments or whatever else, I knew the look she made when things weren't going well, and right now, she wasn't wearing it. In other words, she was convinced she still had this in the bag.

Next, perhaps because she'd cycled through the elements enough times to satisfy her, Lorraine cast a different spell. At first, I thought it was a Fotiá Volídas, but upon closer inspection, there was a chunk of rock in the center of it.

There were spells that launched flaming boulders, but it didn't seem like this was one of them. The reason was because the boulders in those spells would be red-hot by the fire that enveloped them, but the rock in whatever Lorraine had cast was still earthy in color.

Lorraine was more than capable of making that kind of spell adjustment if she wanted to, but I didn't think that had been the case here. As for why, it was because Fuana, the target of the spell, dodged it instead of erasing it like she'd done with all the others. If that had been a regular flaming boulder spell, I doubted she would've had to do that.

As I was pondering that, I looked at the old man.

He nodded. "That was clever."

He must have seen my quizzical look, because he elaborated.

"That can't have been a flaming boulder spell. I dare say it was a Fotiá Volídas layered over a Vráchos Volídas."

I nodded to myself. That was one of the explanations I'd been considering too, but I still wasn't exactly sure what the point of it was.

The old man continued. "In short, it was a two-spell combination. If Fuana wanted to erase it…"

That was enough for me to connect the rest of the dots myself. "Oh, I get it. Since it's two spells, it'd take her extra time."

"Correct. What's more… Well, this is just a guess, but from the way Fuana was discharging her mana earlier, I think the weak points in Fotiá Volídas and Vráchos Volídas are considerably far apart. When combined together, aiming for both in a single moment must be quite difficult."

So basically, it was like trying to pierce the hearts of two animals with a single arrow while hunting. Not even a master at their craft would be able to do that. No wonder Fuana was forced to dodge out of the way. That was a surprisingly simple-to-exploit loophole in her ability. She could still get a lot done before her opponent discovered that, of course, but maybe all the ability amounted to in the end was being a first-encounter killer.

As I was thinking it over, the old man added, "Still, there aren't many folk out there who can do that. Even if you only use simple spells, layered magic is an advanced technique that consumes a taxing amount of mana. It's a double-edged sword that can harm the caster if they let their control over it slip. You'd have to be awfully confident in your spell control to use it in a real fight."

Wearing a lot of mana-amplifying objects at once was *supposed* to cause them to interfere with each other and explode, but Lorraine was the kind of woman who wore them anyway, so…

Despite how she appeared, I thought that maybe "reckless" was a better word for her than "confident," but for the sake of Lorraine's dignity, I figured I'd keep quiet. Because while she definitely *had* the control, it was also true that sometimes her mad schemes made me want to ask her if she was all right in the head.

That said, regarding this current fight against Fuana, I thought Lorraine had made the correct choice. A combination of two or more spells would protect their individual weak points, so Fuana wouldn't be able to make full use of her ability. Running would be her only option.

The fight continued like that for a while, and I began to think this would be an overwhelming victory for Lorraine. But then she cast another Fotiá Volídas and Vráchos Volídas combination, and Fuana stood her ground and faced it.

Was she going to try and erase it? I'd thought that was impossible. However, what Fuana did was something new. This time, she kept her hand closed, formed a fist, and aimed it straight at the incoming spell. She then punched straight forward, and with a loud *bang*, struck the flame-encased chunk of rock dead-on. Her fist caved all the way into the rock...and then the spell vanished.

It was abundantly clear that Fuana had just erased it. The way she'd done it was pretty much entirely by brute force, and I wasn't sure it was sustainable, but the old man looked as though he'd expected this to happen. He'd explained to us earlier that something similar to this might happen, so I doubted Lorraine had been caught off guard. As for what "this" meant...

"Fuana's a mage, but she's also a magic brawler," the old man said. "As you just saw, her weapons are her fists."

From that point on, Fuana's movements changed. Her reactions hadn't been slow when Lorraine had been firing spells at her earlier, but neither had they been especially fast. Now, however...

Fuana kicked off the ground and closed the distance with Lorraine. It was like the final pounce of a carnivorous predator chasing its prey: powerful and intense.

If Lorraine had been a herbivore, you could imagine that she would have panicked, run, and ended up pinned to the ground in what would have been her final moments. She wasn't prey though. She was a hunter that used her intellect and exceptionally quick wits to herd predators into traps.

As Fuana closed in on her, Lorraine calmly watched as though merely obeying her natural instincts. Then, just before her opponent's fist reached her, she threw up a shield spell to protect herself.

Of course, Fuana still had her ability. Even though a shield spell was intrinsically uniform in strength, there would still be minor mana deviations within it. Evidently, she could see the weak point created by those distortions too.

With a *crack*, Lorraine's shield shattered before Fuana's fist touched it, but it took more than that to get the better of a woman like Lorraine.

Fuana immediately went to pull her fist back, but she couldn't. No matter how hard she pulled, it wouldn't move, and her eyes widened in surprise. I looked closer and saw that the shield spell had surrounded her arm like shackles, restraining it in midair.

The shield Lorraine had cast earlier must have been double-layered. A fragile, obvious-to-see one to bait Fuana into lowering her guard, and a second one to open up and clamp back down on where she punched through the first, to restrain her movements.

That had been Lorraine's plan for her spells, and it had worked. Fuana was locked in place. That wasn't to say Fuana couldn't attack with the rest of her body, since only her hand was trapped, but it wasn't Lorraine's fighting style to get in close anyway.

Lorraine, seeing that Fuana couldn't move, smiled and began concentrating her mana. She then aimed at Fuana's arm and fired a thick bolt of lightning. It gave off a loud crackling sound, and Fuana spasmed violently before beginning to fall toward the ground. For a moment, I thought that Lorraine had won, but then I reconsidered. I wasn't sure that would be enough to take Fuana down.

Fuana, who was falling backward, did a quick flip, landed on her feet, and jumped back to create distance from Lorraine. Smoke rose from her smoldering body, and you couldn't call her completely unharmed, but she hadn't lost her fighting spirit. Her eyes still blazed with fiery light like those of a carnivorous animal. It was obvious that Fuana was still raring to go.

Out of everybody, Lorraine seemed the most pleased to realize that. The look she was giving Fuana said: "I'd be disappointed if you went down that easily."

This was definitely a match worth watching.

"If she could move like that, she should've done so from the beginning," I murmured.

"She does start out like that sometimes," the old man replied. "But she must have thought it wouldn't work on Lorraine."

"In what sense?"

"Lorraine's a mage, but she's quite capable with close-quarter combat, no?"

"I guess so…" I gave a vague answer since I didn't want to give away any specifics.

The old man caught on and only nodded in response before continuing. "In which case, it's not hard to imagine she'd have defenses prepared to handle a sudden charge from the outset of the match. And even if she didn't, well, you saw what she could do with those shields."

"That makes sense. I spar against her sometimes, and whenever I run at her recklessly, she can deal with it more often than not."

I still sparred against Lorraine, even after my body had become undead. It was fundamentally for both of our training, but to her, it was also experimentation. Ever since I'd become an undead, I'd been developing new abilities on a regular basis. In our spars, we could test the extent of those changes mid-combat.

One example of that was Division, where the me of today would have a better handle on it than the me of yesterday. It wasn't a big difference though—just stuff like being able to extend my patch of darkness a smidgen farther, or being a fraction of a second faster. In a fight, however, that could be huge. Victory was decided in the quickest of instants, after all.

"I believe Fuana dislikes such recklessness," the old man said.

"That's surprising," I replied. "I had her pinned as the type who *only* made reckless moves."

"Despite appearances, she does her thinking where it counts. Although I suppose that's something else she does instinctively, so maybe you *could* say she doesn't think at all, but that's semantics. At any rate, she was likely trying to catch Lorraine off guard."

Now that he mentioned it, I thought he was probably right. "Good point. If I was a mage and my opponent made it seem as if she could only move like a mage, I'd be taken aback if she suddenly came at me like that."

That must have been what Fuana had been aiming for. Currently, she was moving around the arena as freely as she pleased. It was less magic and more the movements of a beast. Most people would never expect a small girl clad in oversized robes like her to be capable of moving like that.

It went without saying that judging a book by its cover wasn't a good thing to do, but at the end of the day, appearance was always the first thing people formed impressions from.

The old man nodded. "Indeed. Although, she seems to have failed at it. Lorraine was quick to see through her ability. She must have been forced to discard her plan and resort to her fists."

In other words, Lorraine currently had the upper hand. To prove that, although it looked as if she was the one being pressed right now, Fuana's attacks had yet to breach her defenses.

I wondered if that meant this would be over soon…

"Is this all?" Lorraine asked, looking straight into the eyes of her opponent. They hadn't lost their fighting spirit, even though the girl's body was scorched. "I'll be settling this soon then."

It was hard to tell from appearances which of them was the villain in this scenario. Lorraine was a virtuous adventurer and Fuana was a member of an assassin's organization, so perhaps you could call the latter the evil one, but currently, Lorraine looked like a villainess from every perspective—like a witch who was looking down her nose at an innocent young girl and slowly driving her into a corner.

"This isn't over yet!" Fuana shouted, then kicked off of the ground.

Lorraine knew that her opponent's body should have taken considerable damage from her lightning, but the girl moved so fast that she couldn't tell at all. She was on Lorraine in an instant, her fist already mid-swing, but Lorraine was protected by a countless number of shield spells. Although Fuana's fist smashed through them, one by one, she recast them just as fast—no, *faster*—preventing the girl's attack from ever reaching her. And that wasn't all.

"Barqharba Sijn."

Her offense wasn't lacking either. As she finished her chant, ten spears of lightning appeared from the sky and slammed into the ground, encircling Fuana. The sky above was still clear, and Fuana made to leap up and escape, but before she could, more lightning manifested and completed the prison. Then…

"Shikhrér," Lorraine murmured.

The spears of lightning surrounding Fuana crackled, then began to strike inward. The lightning crashed like torrential rain. With no space to dodge, all Fuana could do was allow it to slam into her body. Almost nobody could receive such an offensive and still remain standing, but to Lorraine's surprise, after a dozen or so seconds of incessant lightning strikes passed and the prison dissipated, Fuana rushed at her with tremendous vigor.

"Oh?" Lorraine said, intrigued. "You endured that? I'd thought it'd hit you directly, but apparently not."

"Hmph," Fuana replied. "Thanks for *giving* me your spell!"

"What?!"

She tried to determine the meaning behind the words, but Fuana's fist was already coming at her. For a moment, it seemed foolish to Lorraine—the girl was repeating the exact same attack again—but that thought was immediately dashed when the blow connected.

"Ngh!"

For the first time, Fuana's fist smashed through all of Lorraine's shields. Then it slammed straight into her arm. Although Lorraine did her best to mitigate the blow, ultimately, she was a mage. Even though she'd strengthened herself physically with mana, it wasn't enough to make her impervious to the strike. She immediately leaped back and put space between her and Fuana, but her arm...

"It feels a little...numb."

It felt like it had been hit by lightning. She studied Fuana, who was chasing after her to make a follow-up attack and saw that the girl's body was *clad in crackling lightning*. That was...

As her thoughts raced, Fuana threw another punch. It broke through her shields again, but she'd expected it this time, and she had a rough grasp on its strength. She recast even more shields, increasing their intensity, and successfully prevented the fist from reaching her.

Fuana didn't give up. She twisted her body and slammed a roundhouse kick straight into the opening her fist had just vacated. It smashed through the remaining shields and blew Lorraine away. Fuana didn't let her go though; the girl kicked hard off the ground and flew into the air, closing distance.

"This is the end!" Fuana somersaulted mid-flight, then launched into a diving kick down toward Lorraine.

*I knew it*, Lorraine thought, fascinated. *That's definitely lightning on her leg.*

"But it's incomplete," Lorraine murmured.

She fired a Fotiá Volídas midair to adjust her trajectory and push herself out of the way of Fuana's dive kick. She reached the ground first, took aim at Fuana, who had still yet to land, and then...

"Barák Seará!"

Lightning formed a sphere that encased Fuana; then it mixed with wind and struck and slashed inward in a violent tempest.

Fuana screamed.

The spell lasted roughly ten seconds. However, that was ten seconds spent within the full might of the storm's fangs. At the end, Fuana, smoking and smoldering, fell from the air and crashed into the ground.

Lorraine looked at the old man, and he descended into the arena to check on Fuana.

"She's still alive," he said. "Don't worry. Her sturdiness is her one redeeming feature. Oh, but before I forget: the winner is…Lorraine!"

"You adapted quite excellently," the old man said to Lorraine as they both returned to the stands. He sounded impressed. "Even I didn't know Fuana could do that."

"Are you talking about how she clad herself in lightning?" Lorraine asked.

"Mmm. I haven't a clue what that was."

"I'm not entirely sure either, but I believe she repurposed the spell I cast on her and used it as armor. It must be an original spell of hers. Her 'Spellwise' title might not be entirely off the mark."

"Ho? It was that impressive?"

As I listened to their conversation, a thought occurred to me. "But you took her out with that Barák Seará at the end, right? If she can wear the spells of others, why didn't she do it with that one?"

"Without asking her, I can't say for sure," Lorraine replied, "but it seemed like her spell was still incomplete. She wore my lightning, yes, but after I took a closer look I noticed she was still being hurt by it. Her wounds were increasing by the moment and her mana expenditure shot through the roof. Still, the idea itself is fascinating. The spell looks simple, but I think it's actually quite deep. I'd love to do some research into it myself."

"Ngh…"

After a while, Fuana woke up. Her injuries had mostly healed already, since Lorraine had doused her with a potion she'd had on hand.

Although Lorraine would probably get mad at me for saying it out loud, I thought maybe she'd done it because she would've felt bad leaving a young girl wounded and burnt all over.

Lorraine then murmured, "It'd set me back if she lost her ability to cast that spell because of this."

That was Lorraine for you—never afraid to be herself. But even if Fuana *did* become unable to use that spell where she wore the magic of others like armor, Lorraine had already seen it once.

With her magic eyes, she'd likely seen through the spell's structure to a certain extent already, so it probably wouldn't be much of a setback. That said, since it was still imperfect, the creator's thought process and input would no doubt be valuable.

I figured Lorraine had already taken all of that into account for her decision to heal Fuana. And maybe, just maybe, part of it *had* been because she hadn't wanted to leave a young girl injured. Despite appearances, Lorraine was a kind woman at heart. So long as experiments weren't concerned, anyway.

Fuana slowly got up and examined her surroundings, before muttering, "I lost. You even made me use my Spelldrain Armor."

"Are you feeling okay?" Lorraine asked. "I applied a potion to your injuries, so they're mostly gone, but I can't say the same for any internal damage you might have suffered. Here, you should drink this just in case."

She handed Fuana another potion. Its blue tinge didn't exactly make it look very appealing, but Lorraine's potions were fairly tasty.

Potions could vary in taste quite a lot depending on who brewed them. Ingredients mattered too, but the brewer was the one who decided what aspects to focus on. Some only cared about making its restorative effects as efficient as possible—which was extremely logical, if you ask me—and some figured that if they were going to be making a drink anyway, it might as well be an enjoyable one. Lorraine was one of the latter kind of brewers, and she valued both taste and efficiency.

Fuana took the proffered potion and just stared at it for a while.

"Don't worry. There's no poison in it," the old man said. "If they wanted to kill you, they've already had any number of chances to do so."

Fuana nodded, looking convinced, and began gulping it all down.

"That was good," she said after she finished. She sounded unhappy about that, but her expression was one of satisfaction. She was looking hale and hearty now too, compared to her previous, slightly ill appearance. Probably because the potion had spread through her body and healed up her insides. Since the first one had only been splashed on her, it wouldn't have had much of an effect on her organs and the like.

That was where magic and divinity surpassed potions. Healing spells and purifying rites would affect the whole body at once, while a potion began from the spot where it was applied, then slowly permeated outward. The deeper you went into the body, the weaker a potion's restorative effect. You had to drink it if you wanted to avoid that from happening, but in the middle of a fight, or if you were trying to give it to a person who was unconscious like with Fuana just now, that was a difficult task.

Still, it wasn't all downsides; potions, once brewed, could be used by anybody. Moreover, so long as you were careful with how you stored them, they'd last as long as their constituent ingredients would. Healing spells or purifying rites were only available for as long as their caster had the strength to use them. All in all, both options had their advantages and disadvantages.

"I'm glad that you seem to be doing fine," Lorraine said. "Now, onto the main topic…"

"Mmm," Fuana replied. "You want to meet the chief, right? Then—"

"No, I was talking about the original spell you used earlier. You called it 'Spelldrain Armor,' I think."

Wait, what did she mean by "no"? We *were* here to meet the chief, and I was willing to bet that I wasn't the only one present who sorely wanted to point that out. However, Lorraine's curiosity had been piqued, and there was no stopping her.

"I have a rough grasp of the structure, but I have few questions," she continued. "Also, it's clearly still an incomplete spell. I could tell by the difficulty you had trying to control it, as well as the fact that it was injuring your body. But I think it has astounding potential, and once it's complete, it will no doubt be a formidable weapon for us mages. Now, I have a number of hypotheses I want to pose to you, so…"

"U-Uh…"

Fuana looked a little put off, but once Lorraine got like this, there was nothing I could do to stop her. We'd just have to wait until she was satisfied. So when the old man and Goblin looked at me, all I could do in response was shake my head.

After a while…

"I get what you're trying to say," Fuana said. "You want me to teach it to you. But the spell's important to me, you know. I can't just give it out for free."

Lorraine nodded emphatically. "Of course. New inventions should be fairly compensated for. What would you like? Money? I'll pay as much as you want. Or maybe magic? Would you like to know some forbidden spells? Or ancient ones? I'd be happy to teach you."

Lorraine really wasn't holding back.

Even though Fuana had asked for payment in the first place, she looked bewildered, like she hadn't expected to be offered so much.

She evidently still wanted it though, because she said, "Th-Then… teach me the spell you used that hurt gramps so badly. That will do."

Perhaps she thought that Lorraine would back down if she asked for such powerful magic.

However, Lorraine didn't hesitate to give her reply. "Sure. Do you want to start now? It was more than one spell though, so it might take you some time to learn it all. Oh, I suppose I should give you a demonstration. I'll borrow the arena for a moment, if that's all right."

Then she headed down into the arena. Goblin was quick on the uptake—without a word, he quickly ran over to reactivate the mana barrier.

I'm sure you can guess what happened next. Lorraine put on a grand magic show, consisting of the three spells she'd used to do a number on the old man. The destructive energy and sheer scale of them made the mana barrier shudder worryingly.

Fuana's jaw was wide open as she watched on in silent shock. She *was* watching though, and I figured the mage in her was properly eager to learn—

"There's no way I'm learning those any time soon…"

Or not. Still, a promise was a promise, and since she'd answered Lorraine's questions about her spell, I figured she was sincere about fulfilling her end of the bargain.

As we watched Lorraine cast her magic, I heard a voice from behind me.

"She's something else. I guess she'd have to be, since she beat Gilli."

"Gilli?" I replied absentmindedly, still watching Lorraine. "Who's that?"

"Oh, he didn't tell you his name? Would you get it if I said 'Spriggan'? His real name's Gilli Flood. There's a city in the south famous for its competition fighting, and there he's known as 'Gilli the Monster.' I recruited him, established the organization...and that's how we ended up where we are now. I feel bad about what happened, by the way. Toward your party and his unit. The person I installed to be our agent in the royal circles double-crossed us, you see. Gave us nothing but skewed info. Came back as soon as I could, but everything's already chaos. Don't even have the time to handle my guild work."

Until about halfway through, I'd only been listening with half a mind because I'd thought it was just Goblin returning. But then I'd realized whoever this was sounded different, and *then* the contents of what they were saying finally registered with me.

I turned around, and as I'd expected, it wasn't Goblin. It was a man whose age was hard to tell. He wasn't young, and I'd have guessed he was over fifty, but I couldn't narrow it down any further than that. His physique wasn't that large—it was more or less average, for an adventurer—but I could tell even through his clothes that he'd forged it well.

What was more, although he was calmly sitting in a spectator's seat like nothing was amiss, I couldn't see any openings in him at all. I immediately knew that I'd stand no chance against him in a fight. I didn't even think I could run. He had a dangerous aura that warned me I would lose my head before I could make it any decent distance away. Despite all of that, the look on his face was cheerful, or maybe you could call it fearless. Whatever it was, it wasn't unpleasant.

I kind of liked him. There was something to him that just drew others in. Still, I had more important things to be concerned with right now.

"Who are you?" I asked.

My voice came out calm and detached, but I was anything but. Panicking would've gotten me nowhere though. I hadn't noticed the man approaching me at all. If he'd decided to attack, I wouldn't have been able to react.

Plus, I couldn't even imagine myself escaping a head-on fight against him, much less winning one. And that was taking into account my current body. In short, both instinct *and* logic were telling me that panicking would be meaningless.

"Me? I'm—"

The man seemed entirely happy to answer me, but before he could, Vaasa sat up groggily in a seat behind him.

"Ngh... Wh-Where am I...?"

Then Vaasa saw the man between us. His eyes popped open wide and he scrambled to kneel at the man's feet.

"Ch-Chief! Wh-What are you doing in a place like this?"

Ah. So this was their chief. I was completely willing to believe that. The man's presence, magnetism, and composure—only a truly exceptional kind of person could possess what he had. *I* could tell as much, and my insight and ability to judge people were basically nonexistent. Anybody would get a similar impression from him.

The man looked disappointed that Vaasa had stolen his introduction, but he faced me and plowed on anyway.

"There you have it. I'm the chief of this organization. The name's Jean Seebeck. Pleasure to meet you."

Just like that. And now that he'd given me his name, I had to give him mine too, right? Him being the chief of an assassin organization didn't mean I could forget my manners. Actually, perhaps it was even the opposite—his position made my inner nature as an underling show itself.

That was a joke.

"I'm Rentt, a Bronze-class adventurer," I said. "I'm here because...I came with my companion to meet you."

"I know. Still, Bronze, huh? Vaasa here's as good as Silver, you know. Close to Gold, even, if he uses his ability. Well, maybe not *that* good, especially in a straight fight. Still, neither is he lackadaisical enough to be beaten by a Bronze."

The man was talking to me, but Vaasa, who was to one side, listening, had a happy gleam in his eyes. It was almost childish of him, but maybe that just spoke to how much he idolized his chief. The man certainly seemed like the broad-minded type. It kind of made you want to follow him.

"Did you watch the fights?" I asked.

"I did. There's a spot up above with a view. Then the young lady over there started throwing ancient magic around, so I came down to get a better look. I appreciate the show. It's quite fascinating."

While I doubted Lorraine was used to getting the "young lady" treatment much, there definitely weren't many mages out there who infiltrated assassin organizations and started showing off ancient magic. I could understand why she'd caught the chief's interest.

"You weren't going to stop us?" I asked. "We were fighting without your permission."

"You can fight as much as you want, so far as I'm concerned. Though truthfully, I hadn't noticed until just earlier. Your fight with Vaasa had already started, so I thought it'd be tactless of me to interrupt. I'd have stopped you if it looked like you were going to kill each other, but neither of you seemed like you wanted that."

*I* hadn't wanted to kill Vaasa, that was for sure, but had that really been true for him too? I distinctly recalled that he'd aimed straight for my vitals with his daggers.

"Yeah, I would've stopped just before I did," Vaasa said defensively.

Even if we ignored whether or not that was true, it was all too easy to forget that kind of intention once your blood was up and pumping. Well, whatever, we could just leave it at that.

"Anyway, it was an interesting match," the man said. "I didn't know you had an ability, Rentt. At least, I never received any reports of such while you were in Maalt."

"That would make sense. It's kind of a recent thing."

The man nodded cheerfully. "Ha ha! I see. I suppose these things do happen."

I'd pictured the chief of an assassin organization to be a more menacing, uncompromising person, but he seemed pretty reasonable. Maybe he'd hear us out. Before we got to that, though, I recalled that I'd heard something kind of crazy, so I figured I'd ask about that first.

"Hey," I said.

"Yes?"

"Isn't Jean Seebeck...the name of the grand guildmaster?" I'd thought the name had sounded familiar, but it had only just come to me where I'd heard it before.

"Yep, that's right," the man replied casually.

From deep down, a thought struck me: *Okay... This is really, really bad.*

Was I going to get out of this alive?

"So, um, could you please let us leave here alive?"

Now that things had come to this, I decided I'd just ask in the most direct way I could think of. Being indirect about it and getting a vague answer would be a pain, and if he wasn't going to let us leave, I figured he'd probably be honest about it.

Chief Jean's eyes widened and he burst into laughter. "Pfft! Is that what you were worried about? Relax; you'll be leaving in one piece. You're Wolf's favorite, aren't you? Who knows what he'll do to me if I vanish you."

That piqued my interest. "Does Wolf know you're…?"

Jean shook his head, anticipating my question. "No, he doesn't. I wouldn't mind telling him, really, but that'd only increase his workload. You know how serious he is about his job, despite how he might seem. Can't go making things harder on him…though that's a little rich, coming from me."

So Wolf didn't know that Jean was the chief of this organization. That was surprising; I thought he would have. Or maybe he really did and just acted like he didn't? That was the kind of man Wolf was. I guess I'd never know without asking him directly…but it was best not to poke my nose too far into these things. I had an extremely strong hunch that it would kick up more trouble than I needed. I didn't want to get saddled with more than what I already had to deal with, so I'd just feign ignorance as much as I could.

Oh, wait, was this exactly how Wolf felt? I supposed I'd never know for sure. Not unless something went terribly wrong.

"I guess that's true," I said. "By the way, I'm here on orders from him to come pick you up. I know you might have your hands full with the organization, but it'd be great if you could finish up your work and come with us to Maalt."

"You don't say? First I'm hearing about this. I actually gave out orders to contact Wolf and tell him to come see *me*. I wanted to get more details on what's happening over in Maalt."

"Are you talking about the dungeon?"

"Yeah. The Tower and the Academy are there too right now, aren't they? You might think that has nothing to do with you and your companions, but you'd be wrong, you know."

Hmm? Wait, what? What did that have to do with the reason we were targeted by assassins?

Jean paused. "We can get to that later. There's a lot I need to explain to you, and I imagine you have a decent amount to tell me too. Let's take this elsewhere. Best if everyone's caught up at once, no?"

Jean pointed to Lorraine and the others in the arena. I nodded, headed down the spectator stands, and beckoned everybody to come over.

"I didn't sense him at all…" Lorraine murmured to me.

She was looking at Jean, who was walking ahead of us, leading the way through the colosseum's hallways. We ascended to ground level, then kept going up. According to Jean, his office was on the highest floor, which also had rooms for royalty and nobility that offered a spacious view of the aboveground arena.

Common folk could spectate from those rooms too, but if you wanted to do that, you had to pay a year's worth of rental fees for it. When I heard how much that was, I firmly decided that spectating from the stands was *much* better. I kind of felt like the noble rooms,

THE UNWANTED UNDEAD ADVENTURER

while very posh-feeling because of their location, were a bit too far to get a good view of the fights. Though, since they had magic viewing equipment, they probably had it better anyway. Still, I personally preferred watching fights in the flesh, with my own two eyes. Was that plebeian of me? It was anyone's guess.

"I didn't notice him either," I said. "And neither did Spriggan."

The ones following Jean right now were me, Lorraine, and Spriggan. The other three—Goblin, Vaasa, and Fuana—stayed in the underground arena. Fuana said she wanted to practice the ancient magic Lorraine had taught her, and Vaasa was going to act as her target dummy. Goblin was operating the arena's mana barriers.

Apparently, it was questionable whether Fuana would be able to get the hang of Lorraine's spells, so since Lorraine had pointed out flaws in her Spelldrain Armor which could be fixed immediately, Fuana had said she was going to be doing that as well.

Despite appearances, she seemed to be quite the researcher, just like Lorraine. From her personality, and her entrance earlier, I'd somewhat made light of the whole "Spellwise" thing, but now that I'd revised my opinion of her, I realized that maybe the title wasn't so far from the truth.

"Didn't notice a thing," Spriggan said. "Can't help that though. It's the chief. You should hear what I had to go through when I joined the organization."

"You were searching for work that wasn't just brawling, weren't you?" I asked. "Looking for companions."

That had been my impression, but I was a little off the mark.

"That's not exactly wrong, but those things weren't so simple to find for me. I made a living fighting in arenas while I looked for more ordinary work. But one day, a strange man called out to me. Asked me if I'd like to make the best of my strength. Got a lot of offers like that at the time, asking me to become their lackey. From the leaders of bandit gangs to nobles who wanted an errand boy. None of that was of any interest to me. But this man was different. Said I'd have a lot of 'colleagues.'"

"By 'colleagues,' you mean…"

"Yes, ability wielders. At the time, I knew my strength was unusual, but I hadn't realized it was a 'unique ability' yet. Nobody exactly researched that kind of thing, and most people knew nothing about it in the first place. And back then, my ability was a lot weaker too. I couldn't stay giant for long, and my limbs were usually the most I could manage. Though, my strength was still far beyond an average person's, so I never lost in the arena."

That proved my suspicion that even unique abilities needed training and that they weren't just convenient get-strong-fast tricks. It still sounded as if the old man had been a monstrous outlier in his younger days too though…

"Although," he continued, "I didn't understand what 'colleagues' meant back then, so I turned him down. That's when he wouldn't take no for an answer, beat me up, dragged me somewhere, and taught me what he meant by 'colleagues.' He showed me people who caused supernatural phenomena to occur without the use of mana, spirit, or divinity, and that's when it clicked for me. Afterward, that man, those colleagues, and I formed the organization together…and here I am today."

"Now then, sit, sit. You too, Gilli."

After reaching his office, Jean sat down and beckoned for all of us to do the same.

The soft leather couch was clearly high quality and made it obvious that he earned a comfortable living. Then again, considering he ran a huge establishment like this in the capital, there was no way he *didn't*.

His public work alone had to make a killing. Colosseums were where coin flowed like water. Gambling was allowed, so long as it was reported and approved. Of course, some people did it under the table anyway—mostly the type who made a living in the shadows—but Jean and his organization *were* those people. It was easy to imagine that they made their money above *and* under the table. I wondered if they paid taxes. I kind of doubted it.

We sat on the couch, and Gilli signaled someone who looked like a serving lady. She began to prepare us all drinks.

It was black tea, and from the scent, quite high quality. I wasn't completely unfamiliar with the beverage, since it was a favorite of Lorraine's that I'd shared with her from time to time, but that didn't change the fact that it was expensive. I didn't drink it often. I liked the taste, though.

After making sure everybody had their tea, the serving lady bowed and left the room.

Jean waited for her footsteps to fade away before speaking again. "So...where should I begin?"

Lorraine stopped him. "First things first. Rentt and I came here to ask you—that is, your organization—to not send assassins after us again. Could we settle that before continuing?"

She was being very direct, but she must have decided that was likely for the best when it came to dealing with Jean. After all, during our walk here, I'd given her the gist of the conversation I'd had with him in the spectator stands. I'd also told her about my read on Jean as a person. Naturally, that wasn't conclusive evidence, but it did seem pretty clear that he wasn't planning on killing us. That was probably one of the reasons why Lorraine had been so direct—she'd wanted to confirm that.

"Ah, yes," Jean said. "I suppose we should get that out of the way first. We won't send anyone after you again, of course. I said this to Rentt earlier, but we received faulty intelligence from an internal source. Put simply, we had a spy among the court, but they betrayed us. We believed their information, one thing led to another, and it was determined that you needed to be taken care of."

"Why would…?"

Lorraine sounded as perplexed as I was. Why had things turned out this way? I remembered that the old man had said the organization was aware that the second princess had told us about the scepter and the state of the kingdom. However, that information had come from a diviner. The organization had surmised that we'd been ordered to transport the new scepter, which was why they'd attempted to stop us.

But I wasn't sure *why* they wanted that. Without the scepter, the kingdom would see an increase in the number of undead. Wasn't bringing a new one back a good thing?

I knew that Gisel, the backer of the first princess who'd hired the organization, didn't want the second princess to accomplish the feat and get the credit, but… Well, maybe that really was all there was to it?

"You've heard about the scepter, right?" Jean asked.

"Yes," Lorraine replied. "We were told it was a divine treasure with the ability to dampen unclean energy throughout the kingdom. Would its presence be a problem for your organization? I suppose you'd get more work if the kingdom didn't have it…"

Not only them—adventurers would get more work too. Now that Lorraine had pointed it out, I realized a man in Jean's position had a lot to gain. His day job running the adventurer's guild and side job running the organization would see an influx of business.

However, Jean shook his head. "No, that's not the case. I can't deny that's what the result would be, but we put more than enough bread on the table with what we handle already. Although, I can't say the idea doesn't have a little appeal to me. In certain ways, it would dramatically improve the lives of adventurers. Well, the lower-class ones, that is."

As matters stood, skilled adventurers could already earn a decent income, but lower-class ones similar to my old self and Rina barely made enough to guarantee themselves a bed to sleep in for the night. On the other hand, if the number of undead monsters were to increase, so would the amount of bounties put out on them, which could alleviate that problem. More of the weakest class of undead, such as skeletons—or even small skeletons—meant more available income.

You didn't see those types too much around Yaaran, but that was probably because of the scepter. They were weak monsters, so I doubted it took much for it to purge them. It was a shame that process didn't leave their magic crystals behind, since they were still worth enough to make a living, but there was no use mourning over what never technically existed in the first place.

Still, without the effect of the scepter, those types of undead might pop up more and more. With the boost in income, paying for a roof over your head every night would no longer be an issue. That sounded great—for people like me, that is. For an ordinary person, weak undead were plenty threatening. There was no question that we were all better off without them.

"So...why try to stop a new scepter from being delivered?" Lorraine asked. "Ah, and I should mention that we never accepted that request to begin with, so you wouldn't have needed to assassinate us regardless."

The request that had actually been made of us was to visit the Holy Tree. What purpose that would serve I had no idea, and we hadn't formally accepted yet anyway. I'd made the best of my wits and manners to keep the request a respectful arm's length away, and that was where it still was. There was no way I was going to take it if it meant painting a target on my back for assassins. I wasn't near that strong enough, and I knew it. In fact, I was currently the weakest person in the room...

Now that I'd remembered who I was surrounded by, I found myself feeling kind of down. They made me wonder if I'd really grown stronger at all.

"First," Jean said, "we should establish that the presence of the scepter is preferable to the alternative. It contributes hugely to the peace of Yaaran."

We knew that, of course. I was about to point that out, but Jean held a hand up to stop me and continued.

"However, that is from the perspective of people other than the wielder. The current scepter is draining the king's life, and... Oh? From your lack of surprise, I take it you are already aware?"

Perhaps it had been in-the-know information at the outset, but I got the feeling it was less confidential these days. Then again, we hadn't had a clue until the second princess told us about it...

It was likely that the upper nobility and top brass of the kingdom knew. Maybe that was why Yaaran's royalty was so much more revered than that of other countries. Without them, everyone living in Yaaran would be worse off—not only commoners, but nobles too.

If the undead ran rampant over their territories, who knew how much more expensive it would be to deal with them compared to how things were now? Other countries already bore such costs as a matter of course, so it wasn't as if the kingdom would cease to function, but there was obviously no need to go out of the way to create that burden.

They could always supplant the throne and take the scepter by force, sure…but the high elves had gifted it to the *current* royal family. If they were replaced, I doubted the high elves would be willing to continue maintaining it, or offer available solutions if problems like the current one cropped up. It created a situation where the royal family needed to survive to retain the scepter, even if that meant only as figureheads.

That had me wondering if that was where Yaaran's tranquility—especially among its nobles—came from. It was a surprising thought.

"Yes," Lorraine replied. "The second princess told us."

Jean nodded. "I see. While the king's condition isn't public, it isn't much of a secret either. As for the scepter…its effect is known, but only a select few are privy to its current condition. Considering your positions, I suppose the second princess *is* the only source you could have learned of it from."

"How did you find out?"

"I…technically found out from the spy I mentioned earlier. The scepter itself, Kars showed me in his younger days, but I didn't know of the risk it posed back then. I went to see him as soon as I found out, but he just waved me off and said there was 'no other option,' the fool. Of course he has another damn option."

"Kars"? Wait a minute, was that…?

"By 'Kars,'" Lorraine said, "do you mean…?"

"The king. Karsten Reshon Yaaran. I've known him since he was little snot. I'm his senior by quite a bit, though."

He was older than the king? I thought I remembered the king being sixty-five. Well, given Jean's famous exploits, some simple math put him at over eighty, so I guessed that made sense. He looked way too young for that, though.

Due to the nature of the job, adventurers boasted far greater physical ability and mana reserves than your average person, and that generally made it more difficult for them to age. Even still, Jean was something else. I guessed being a legendary figure meant he was an outlier among adventurers too.

"So?" Lorraine asked calmly. "What did you mean by another option?"

"Fixing the scepter, of course. His condition is only the way it is because it broke in the first place. Still, easier said than done. He's not willing to part with it, not even briefly. And the high elves wouldn't leave the Land of the Venerable Holy Tree even if we bothered asking them. We were looking at a dead end. But then Gisel came out and said that the Tower had found a way to repair the scepter that would be quick *and* that wouldn't require it to be taken out of the king's possession."

Lorraine immediately leaned forward. "How?"

Repairing a broken divine treasure... If such a method really existed, then it would absolutely attract Lorraine's interest. When she got like this, most people would instinctively shy back a little, either afraid or put off.

However, Jean answered her without batting an eye. "The materials that go into the creation of a divine treasure are said to be extremely special. They're nothing like regular magical items. Only after a large number of these precious components are used and the finest crafting techniques are applied can a divine treasure be created. That's why, aside from the ones created directly by the gods, races such as the high elves and dwarves have been known to create them on rare occasions."

I tilted my head. "We know that much, but what are you trying to say?"

"Of those special materials, it is said that one stands head and shoulders above the rest. It is usually impossible to obtain, and the reason so many who seek to create a divine treasure cannot. According to Gisel, the Tower made a breakthrough and discovered what it was. What's more, the once-in-a-lifetime chance to obtain it has arrived. Right now, in this era, in this kingdom."

Lorraine looked disappointed. "That…sounds like a scam. 'The item you want is up for grabs right here, right now! Don't miss out. Make your decision immediately!'"

Jean laughed and nodded. "You're exactly right. But unless you've forgotten, our organization is composed of ability wielders. It's not far-fetched that we'd have someone who could discern if a person is telling the truth, no?"

Lorraine's expression changed again—to realization, this time. The human mind was exceedingly complex, and it was often difficult to tell what somebody was thinking. Forcing a person to do something with magic wasn't easy, and tampering with memories was straight-up impossible, yet we'd seen Siren do just that with her ability.

Ability wielders could do things that magic considered impossible. It wasn't strange in the least for one of them to be able to tell truth from lies.

"Okay," Lorraine said. "So let's assume what Gisel said was true. What is this special material?"

"It is, in fact…" Jean paused, taking his time as though he were unveiling a personal treasure of his. Then, he said it.

*A dungeon core.*

Needless to say, the facial expressions Lorraine and I made were indescribable.

Dungeon cores. They were a dungeon's nucleus and command mechanism. By absorbing and assimilating one, you would gain the ability to control its dungeon. The vampire Laura Latuule had taught us that.

Shumini, another vampire, had once created a dungeon under Maalt, but he hadn't kept the core himself: he'd forced it onto Rina, who he'd made his servant. We had discovered his plans, and Laura had separated it from Rina and absorbed it into herself, where it currently remained.

At a guess, the "once-in-a-lifetime chance" that Jean had heard about from Gisel was that very dungeon core. In which case…

This was a lost cause already, and Lorraine and I both knew it—hence, our expressions. Still, dungeons existed everywhere. Even Maalt had three if you included the new one. There were hundreds out there in the world. If you wanted a dungeon core, it didn't have to come from Maalt. You could just as easily go somewhere else.

Lorraine and I exchanged looks that said we'd hear the rest of what Jean had to say first, then turned back to face him.

"Not exactly the reactions I'd expected," he said. "Oh, do you not know what a dungeon core is? It's not exactly common knowledge, I suppose. I kind of assumed you two would know though…"

Evidently, he'd mistaken our reactions for surprise and confusion. There was no harm in correcting him, really, but I stayed silent, choosing not to interrupt as he continued.

"A dungeon core is exactly what it sounds like—the core of a dungeon. They exist in every dungeon and are often well protected. If you destroy one, the dungeon collapses too. But in truth, none of this information has been verified."

That mostly agreed with what Laura had told us. But if he was saying it hadn't been verified, then why did they believe dungeon cores existed?

Jean must have seen the doubt on my face. "The guild has a long history, and there are a number of stories of people having destroyed one. It's just, none of those stories can be made public. Usually because the cores were in the possession of royalty or the clergy—you get the idea. Apparently, the cores can be taken out of their dungeons. I'm sure you've heard the tales of adventurers who've made it into a dungeon's deepest depths and defeated the fearsome boss monster in the final chamber, right? Well, those guardians—the boss monsters—and the owners of the core are two different things. Think of it like...the relationship between a store's owner and its manager. And the owner doesn't necessarily have to be in the dungeon."

That made sense. It was a pretty mundane analogy, but it got the point across. It got me thinking though. If Laura was currently the dungeon's owner, who was the manager?

I pictured monster employees who dreaded the owner's occasional visits. Skeletons lined up in a row out front to greet her enthusiastically. Goblins and orcs cheerfully rubbing their hands together. Slimes producing beverages for the customers...

Hey, that dungeon sounded kind of fun…provided you could handle the owner biting your neck and draining you of blood if you displeased her. Or crushing you with her gravity magic.

Laura had said she was holding on to four dungeon cores, so did that make her a large company in the dungeon master industry? Considering that assimilating even one was extremely difficult, she was probably at the level of a mega-conglomerate.

"I've got the general idea," Lorraine said. "So where is this dungeon core allegedly going to be, and how will it be retrieved?"

"Maalt's new dungeon," Jean replied.

Lorraine and I exchange looks again. It was just as we'd suspected. Still, Jean had said himself that the owner wouldn't necessarily be in the dungeon. That being the case, he had to know it wouldn't be so easy to obtain the core.

"How do you determine who's holding the core?" I asked. "If they're outside of it, they could be anywhere."

"True, but a newly formed dungeon is different. According to the Tower's experts, new dungeons are still unstable, so the owner of their core needs to remain inside. They've estimated this period to be around a year or more."

That meant that they were working under the premise that the owner was still inside and that turning the place upside down to find and kill them would get them the dungeon core.

Still, that aside…

"That's some impressive analysis by the Tower," Lorraine said. "Dungeon research worldwide hasn't really progressed much, not even in the Empire."

"Pretty much," Jean replied. "Still, discovery is a sudden thing, and you never know where it'll come from. Would you believe the Tower found a way to create a small-scale, artificial dungeon? I do mean 'small' though. Apparently they can only get it as big as an ant's nest and can't harvest cores from it. Who knows how many hundreds of years it'll be before it becomes a practical resource? That said, they showed it to me, and it was definitely a working dungeon. The monsters were only tiny ants...but they could spit acid. That's dangerous in its own right."

"They've progressed so far?! That's wonderful. Yaaran's Tower doesn't have any particularly notable contributions to their name, so I'd thought they were behind the times, but I stand corrected. You wouldn't happen to know the name of the Tower's head dungeon researcher, would you?"

That was a fairly harsh thing to say, but I guessed that didn't make it any less true. As for the name, Lorraine probably wanted to know so she could pick the person's brain later down the line.

Evidently, it was no particular secret, because Jean answered easily, "I do. Hamishy Favor. Unhealthy-looking, and the very picture of what you'd imagine a researcher to be...but brilliant all the same. So much so you can practically feel it."

If the veteran head of two major organizations—one legal and one not—was saying that, then this Hamishy person must really be something else.

Since Yaaran was a backwater kingdom, I'd taken for granted that it'd be mostly behind other countries when it came to advanced research, but finding out that we had someone as talented as that made me kind of happy. It wasn't my achievement, and I wouldn't call myself very patriotic, but the mood just kind of took me.

Still, even a genius's research could be wrong sometimes. In fact, the research had just begun, so mistakes would be the norm. Case in point: it hadn't been a year and Laura was already outside of the dungeon—which would mean that this plan would be doomed to fail from the outset.

Oh no, whatever would we do?

"So the reason the Tower and the Academy are in Maalt right now…" Lorraine said.

Jean nodded. "Yeah. The Tower is looking for the dungeon core. The Academy is too, but they're being backed by the first prince. It's a race to see who finds it first."

"So the prince knows it's necessary to repair the scepter too?" I asked.

"He does," Jean replied. "Gisel purposefully leaked the information. At any rate, the Tower's first priority is to discover a method for finding out who the core's owner is. It's a manpower problem, so they want as many people as possible to help search the dungeon. If the Academy finds it first, the Tower plans to steal it from them."

That was logical, sure, but it would also be bloody. While it was a new dungeon that wasn't all that large, it would still take a considerable amount of time to search every corner of it. It was understandable that they wanted as many people as possible, since the one-year deadline didn't give them much space to work with, but the willingness to fight over it once they found it was a bit much…

Still, from our point of view, we knew where the dungeon core was, so we knew that conflict would never happen. They'd never find Laura *in* the dungeon, and even in the very hypothetical event they realized she was the owner, how would they ever take it from her? I hadn't gotten an up close look at Laura fighting, but what I did see had been enough to tell me how monstrously powerful she was.

On top of that, she was in the Latuule manor, surrounded by her personnel. A single servant was at the very least a middle vampire, and that was just the lowest rung. Most were actually greater vampires.

The Latuule estate had enough military strength to go to war against an entire country. Could the Tower and Academy of a backwater kingdom like Yaaran win against that? Why even bother asking? There was no two ways about it—anything would be better than trying the extremely bad idea of taking the dungeon core from Laura.

If anything, convincing the king to change his mind would be far easier. I could tell Lorraine and I were thinking the exact same thing, but we couldn't exactly come clean to Jean about it.

Since I didn't really have anything else to say on the subject, I decided to change to a topic that was much more important to us.

"Right, I think I'm caught up on the dungeon core. But that doesn't explain why we needed to be killed."

"That would be because the second princess was trying to have the high elves create a new scepter," Jean said. "And we thought you had been chosen to be the couriers."

I did remember the old man saying something along those lines.

"But what's so wrong with that?" I asked. "A new scepter would mean the king wouldn't have to use the old one. I don't see a problem."

"That's true. But the second princess wasn't going to hand the scepter over to the king. She was going to wait until the old one had drained him to death, then use the new one to seize the throne."

"No way," I said immediately. "She isn't the type to do something like that. At least, she didn't seem like it to me."

"And you're right. That's the faulty information I mentioned, passed to us by the spy we had among the court. The organization acted accordingly, and I wasn't here at the time to catch it since I was on business elsewhere. There was nobody around who knew the second princess well enough. The specifics of the scepter hadn't been passed down to most of them either, so nobody could make an accurate judgment call. One thing led to another, and Gilli got ordered to kill you and foil the second princess's plot. He'd already left by the time I came back, so I couldn't put a stop to it."

The old man in question looked shocked. "The order came from the vice chief, so I didn't think to question it…"

"It seems the vice chief had been in Gisel's pocket since a long time back. I've already taken care of it though. We've got a vice chief no longer, and no court spy either."

That was a terrifying thing to say so casually. Forget "no longer in the organization." He'd probably meant "no longer in the world of the living."

I guessed that was what Jean had been busy with recently. Chief of a shadow organization or not, political power struggles couldn't be easy to deal with. Still, one thing was bugging me.

"You never noticed your vice chief was working for Gisel?"

That was a pretty big oversight to make…

"I've got no excuses. That said, the organization wasn't always this big. We grew little by little by taking apart and assimilating other outfits. One was the vice chief's. Imagine keeping a secret like that for thirty years, without even tipping your direct subordinates off. Honestly, it's more impressive than anything else."

So the vice chief had kept the secret their entire life, waiting for the critical moment and working diligently without telling their colleagues or subordinates. No wonder nobody had thought to be suspicious.

In the end, the result had been failure. It seemed a sad sort of life to have lived, but if the person themselves had been glad to sacrifice themselves for their loyalty, then perhaps it wasn't so bad. Even though they'd been the perpetrator who'd caused us such trouble, they were definitely a person of principle, in a way, so I found myself feeling a little melancholy.

Maybe I could only think like that because I'd never met them and we'd come out of their plot no worse for wear. If we'd been truly hurt in some way, I probably would have held a bitter grudge against them.

"So, if that's the case," I began, "what are you going to do now? From the look of things, Gisel's throwing caution to the wind and doing everything she can to put the first princess on the throne. Are you going to keep working with her?"

"No, our contract with her is concluded. I'd be perfectly content with the second princess bringing a new scepter back. I know she'd willingly hand it over to the king. The problem is whether she can manage to get it. How's that looking, anyway?"

"I'm afraid we can't tell you that," Lorraine said. "I know we've been frank with each other so far, but we do have certain matters of confidentiality to keep."

We didn't actually, especially considering we hadn't even accepted the princess's request, but Lorraine was likely thinking that involving ourselves any further in royal matters would be bothersome.

The stance she was taking was basically: "You handle the rest. We have nothing to do with this."

I completely agreed with that. I didn't want to see undead popping up all over Yaaran, but if we poked our noses any deeper into the scepter problem, we'd be risking our lives.

Risking mine was one thing, but it was Lorraine's and Augurey's that were the concern here. Besides, even if that wasn't the case, it was still best to avoid attracting the attention of the kingdom's heavyweights like Gisel.

If my adventurer class was higher, maybe I'd be able to show off and declare that it was an adventurer's job to uphold the peace of the kingdom, but as things stood, I had my hands full taking care of my own problems.

Now that there was no longer a threat of Jean's organization coming after us, I was satisfied. The best step to take next would be to wish him luck and wave goodbye.

Or it would be, if we didn't need Jean to come to Maalt with us.

This was a problem.

"Makes sense," Jean replied. "I'll go ask for an audience with the second princess tomorrow."

He backed off relatively easily. It did sound like he was an acquaintance of the second princess after all. The king too. The confidence in his words probably came from the fact that it wouldn't be much trouble for him to meet them whenever he pleased.

"That would be the surest method," Lorraine said. "As for our other purpose, do you have any plans to visit Maalt?"

If he didn't want to go, we could just get him to write a letter to that effect and be done with it.

Thinking back, Wolf hadn't seemed too enthused about the idea of Jean paying a visit either. I wondered if he'd actually celebrate him not coming.

Contrary to my expectations, Jean said, "Yeah, I do. Been thinking it's due time I stopped by. Tomorrow's...not open for me since I'll be seeing the princess like I mentioned, but how about we head for Maalt the day after? That sound good?"

"Are you sure?" I asked. "Aren't you busy?"

Jean had a mountain of issues to handle. He not only had the organization to deal with, but the guild and the scepter business too. I had my own affairs, such as reporting back to Hathara and preparing for the Silver-class exam, but they were all personal matters. They paled in comparison to Jean's responsibilities.

"The scepter issue isn't going to be solved in a handful of days," Jean replied. "And I don't want to see the dungeon core secured before that happens. I'd like to check on the Tower and the Academy's progress. I suppose I have a personal interest too. The Tower's artificial one aside, even I've never seen a newly formed dungeon before. I'm curious about what it's like."

It was abundantly clear to myself and Lorraine that they couldn't have made any progress, but we couldn't tell him that. It'd only lead to him asking us how we knew.

Even if we did want to explain, we would have to be extremely careful. They had an ability wielder who could tell when somebody was lying. The best way to avoid that scrutiny was to direct the conversation so that we wouldn't be scrutinized in the first place.

Jean's proposal wasn't a bad one for us anyway. We had, after all, been tasked with bringing him back to Maalt. Maybe Wolf preferred carrying on without Jean, but there was no reason for us to be so considerate of him. He was the one who'd pushed this job on us, so the least he could do was take responsibility for it.

"All right," Jean said. "Let's go with that then. We head for Maalt the day after tomorrow. That okay?"

"Sure," I replied. "In the meantime, we'll get our own preparations ready. Regarding the wagon..."

"We'll take care of it," Lorraine said. "So you won't need to make any arrangements. We'll see you in two days."

With that, our talks were over.

After we returned to the inn and told everything to Augurey, he sighed.

"Ha. This has gotten awfully complicated, hasn't it? It's not often one gets dragged into a mess like this. I don't know whether to call it a novel experience or just plain bad luck."

Siren had gone back with Spriggan to the organization, so Lorraine, Augurey, and I were alone.

The decrease in numbers made things feel calmer, but also a little lonely. Even though they'd come after our lives, we'd also been through danger together, so I'd grown fond of Spriggan's group. Now that they were gone, I couldn't help but feel a little down. Then again, while I wanted to think that we wouldn't try to kill each other again since we weren't enemies anymore, they worked for a shadow organization. It wasn't out of the realm of possibility that they'd come up against us in the future. Given what Jean and Spriggan had said, though, I could probably feel safe that they'd make arrangements to ensure that didn't happen.

"Definitely bad luck," Lorraine said. "That's what I'd like to say, at least, but we got a lot out of it too. I suppose you could say we came out even."

She'd acquired a new spell formula and had her eyes opened to the latent potential of unique abilities.

Moreover, it was probably an advantage that we'd made acquaintances in a far-reaching shadow organization, regardless of whether we could actually commission them to work for us. Sure, if we went around blabbing about them, they might come after us again, but as long as we didn't do that, there was always a chance we could call on our connections sometime later down the line.

"That might be looking at it too optimistically," Augurey murmured, "but now that our worries are behind us, maybe that's for the best. Still, I guess this means tomorrow's goodbye. I'm going to miss you two."

I could hear the sincerity in his words. He was right. Augurey was based in the capital, but that wasn't the case for Lorraine and me. We'd get the chance to come back eventually, but at least for a little while, this was goodbye.

# Chapter 4:     The Saint and the Orphanage

The next morning…

"Ah, Rentt and Lorraine. I got a message from the guild saying they wanted you there."

As we were having breakfast, the innkeeper walked past us, leaving us with that brief notice.

"You think it's from Jean?" I asked Lorraine. My mind had immediately jumped to him since he'd made such a strong impression on me yesterday.

Lorraine shook her head. "No, I doubt it. It's probably about the other matter. You know, from a few days ago?"

"Oh! You're right…"

I'd been confused for a moment when she'd said it wasn't Jean, but then I quickly realized what she was talking about. It wouldn't do to keep our client waiting, so we quickly scarfed down our breakfasts and left for the adventurer's guild.

"Welcome. It's good to see you two," the guild employee said. "Now, as for why we sent for you…"

"We know," Lorraine replied. "Elza's request, yes?"

"Ah, you've already talked to her? Yes, that's exactly it. I must say, it's terribly rare to receive a direct appointment from an abbess of the Church of the Eastern Sky, much less one who's also a saint. I do hope you'll see to the request with the utmost care."

The guild employee sounded a touch nervous. I couldn't see the need to feel that way, but then again, we'd met Elza in person. Maybe this was the normal reaction when dealing with a saint.

That'd qualify Lorraine to be a saint too then. Sadly, she wasn't much of one, since the divine spirit that had blessed her had been pretty shabby. Or perhaps the competition was just too stiff. Being upper management in a religious entity that spanned the entire kingdom was kind of hard to beat.

"Of course," Lorraine replied. "Are we picking her letter up here, or…?"

"No, you're to accept it from her directly. I apologize for the inconvenience, but please go to the Ephas Abbey."

It felt like we were being given the runaround, but I supposed that just spoke to the letter's importance. In the first place, going through the guild for this let us earn merit to advance our classes. If anything, the abbess was working around us, so I had no right to complain.

Lorraine and I gave the guild employee a nod and left for the Ephas Abbey.

When we reached our destination, an elderly cleric came running over as soon as he saw us.

"Lorraine and Rentt, I presume?"

We nodded, and he continued.

"We've been awaiting you. Please, come in."

He guided us smoothly inside and, unlike our previous visit, took us straight to the back. Elza must have instructed him to do so.

He showed us to a familiar drawing room, bowed deeply, and left. After a brief lull, there came a knock at the door.

"Come in," Lorraine said.

"Pardon me." The door opened, revealing Abbess Elza. "It's good to see you two again. Have you enjoyed your stay in the capital these past few days?"

We stood to greet her, and she beckoned us to sit back down, taking a seat for herself as she did so.

"I'm afraid we didn't really get the chance," I said. "Most of our time was spent working, so we had little to spare for strolling around the city."

Augurey had been enthusiastic about taking jobs for us. Not that I was complaining, since the end result of his efforts was us getting a payday.

The jobs had bumped me past the requirements to take the Silver-class Ascension Exam too—something that would've taken me a decent amount of time to achieve otherwise, since I mostly took solo Bronze-class requests if left to my own devices. To nobody's surprise, higher-ranked jobs came with more benefits.

"That's a shame," Elza said. "To tell the truth, I was wondering as to your whereabouts. I, in fact, wrote the letter a little while ago and informed the guild to contact me upon your return."

That figured; writing a letter wouldn't exactly take up a whole day. I felt bad we'd made her wait.

"About that," I began. "I'm sorry we—"

Elza hurriedly shook her head, cutting me off. "Oh no! It wasn't my intention to criticize you! I'd simply heard tell of violent disturbances lately, so I was worried that you might have been implicated. I'm relieved to see you're both okay!"

We *had* actually been implicated in a violent disturbance— almost died from it, even—but I wasn't about to tell her that.

Or, wait, was Elza already aware of our circumstances and trying to bait us somehow?

No, that was too paranoid of me. The Church of the Eastern Sky was a vast religious entity that spanned Yaaran, but that hardly made them an all-seeing intelligence organization. And anyway, gathering information on the kingdom, nobles, or big-name merchants was all well and good, but I doubted intelligence on Lorraine and I was worth much.

Our skeletons in the closet aside, we were, for all intents and purposes, regular adventurers. Not the kind of movers and shakers who'd be involved in momentous events. Although, it was getting harder to say that by the day...

"Our apologies for worrying you," Lorraine said. "But as you've seen, we're hale and hearty. We're returning to Maalt tomorrow too, so your letter came at the perfect timing."

"My, tomorrow? Then you truly have lacked the time to see the city's sights."

"I'm afraid so. We do plan on spending the rest of the day going for a stroll though. We need to pick up some souvenirs for our friends in Maalt, and since one of them used to reside here, her requests were rather particular...to the point where I hope we don't end up running in circles trying to fulfill them. Quite honestly, it's enough to make me want to hire a guide."

I was a little concerned too. Lorraine had been to the capital a number of times and had a rough grasp on the lay of the land, but Rina's requests—as expected of a former local girl—had been highly specific. I didn't know if we could get everything for her and our other friends in a single day.

Elza seemed to pick up on our unease, because after a moment's consideration, she said, "My, my. Hmm. In that case, shall I be your guide around the city?"

"You really think this is okay?" I asked.

Lorraine and I were standing in front of the Ephas Abbey, waiting.

She thought to herself for a moment, before saying, "No, not really. But if she says it is…"

I didn't think that was very reassuring. What were we talking about, you ask? Well…

"Oh, there you are! I'm awfully sorry for the wait."

From the vast entrance of the Ephas Abbey came…nobody. She actually stepped out of the small door to the side, her head on a swivel as she walked.

"She" was, of course, Abbess Elza Olgado, the person in charge of the very abbey she'd just left. She was dressed in the clothes not of the clergy, but of a regular pedestrian. They were a little out of fashion with the current trend in Yaaran, but they were simple and ubiquitous.

I was far too scared to ask what her actual age was, but in her current getup, she looked the perfect part of a young lady in her early twenties. Despite the fact that I was pretty sure she was in the same generation as Lillian. Which wasn't to say Lillian was old— I genuinely thought she was on the younger side. It was just that her plumpness and motherly aura didn't exactly scream "young" to the senses. If the two walked side by side, I thought they'd come off as similar in age.

"You were in there for quite a while," Lorraine said. "Was everything okay?"

"Oh, I just…had a harder time giving them the slip than I expected. I left word that I'd be leaving though, so I'm sure it'll be fine. Anyway, come on you two. We should hurry before they find us."

Elza grabbed Lorraine and me by the hand and set off at a brisk walk.

Wait, "giving them the slip"? I was sure Lorraine and I were thinking the same thing right now.

*That doesn't sound good.*

"So…you shook off the clergy members who were looking high and low for you and snuck out of the abbey?"

Lorraine was holding her head while we walked, as though she were in pain. She sounded like she was in pain too.

"No, no, you've misunderstood me," Elza replied. "I left a letter stating that I would be out on business for a brief time and did my best to ensure that I didn't obstruct anybody's work on my way out. I'm sure that everybody's quite grateful for my consideration right about now."

To me, that sounded an awful lot like "they're agonizing right around now because they realized they abjectly failed to notice my brilliant escape plan." I was tempted to say as much, but Elza seemed to know already, because she continued.

"Joking aside, it's not uncommon for me to step out and go about the city alone from time to time. It'll be fine. I've taken care of all my work, so my absence shouldn't be missed."

I took that to mean they'd be fine with it since she'd completed her responsibilities. Part of me was still unsure about this, but I was far from an expert on the inner workings of the Church of the Eastern Sky, so I decided to take her word for it.

"That's good to hear then," I said. "But, and I don't mean to be rude, can we really count on you to be our guide around the city?"

Since she was in charge of managing the abbey, I figured there was a chance she wasn't too familiar with the more ordinary parts of the city. Big shots didn't get to go on many outings without their retinue. Her Highness the princess, for example, had likely never walked the streets alone. Just because Elza had been born and raised here didn't necessarily mean she could play the part of guide.

However, Elza said, "Trust me. We'll be fine. I practically lived on these streets as a child. I know them better than anybody…except perhaps Lillian."

"Lillian's from the capital too?" Lorraine asked.

Elza mulled it over for a bit. "More or less, yes. We were childhood friends, her and I. Always together since we were little. And though the timing was slightly different, we chose the same path in life too."

So the two *were* of a similar age. That aside though, I was impressed that two childhood friends had both turned out to be saints. Divinity was considerably rare—not that I'd felt that recently, since I'd been running into its wielders like I was at a divinity bargain sale. Two close friends both being blessed with it barely ever happened. I couldn't talk though, given Lorraine and I both had it. But in our case, it was mostly that the divine spirit who'd blessed us had been the sloppy type. Weak too. Whatever Elza and Lillian had was unmistakably more impressive than ours.

I was about to ask more about their childhood, but Elza spoke up before I could.

"Oh, come to think of it, where did you want to go? I haven't asked yet."

I suspected it had been on purpose, and Lorraine was looking at me and shaking her head too. I didn't feel the need to press the issue, so I gave up on asking my question and handed Elza the small notebook Rina had given us.

It would technically be classified as a dubious tome penned by an undead, but at least no evil spirits would come rushing out to attack when you opened it. I'd already checked the contents and confirmed there was nothing in there that was problematic. Unless you counted the sketches of skeletons and vampires scattered throughout it.

"This is rather...blasphemous. A hobby of the two of yours?"

"Definitely not."

"No way."

Both of us denied it, but while Lorraine might have gotten away with that, I was wearing a skull mask, so I didn't really have a leg to stand on. Elza stared at me, and I had to avert my eyes.

It was my loss.

"Not that I mind, really," she said. "That aside, these instructions are quite detailed. It will take us until evening to get to all of these places."

So even with a born and bred city girl's help, it'd take some time. I wasn't too bothered though. We had the whole day free. If there was a problem, it would be...

"We're fine with that, but are you?" I asked. "Do you have the time?"

"It's no problem at all. There is one place I'd like to stop by after we're done though. Could I ask you to accompany me?"

In all likelihood, she didn't need us, but she'd volunteered to be our guide and we had no reason to refuse, so we agreed.

"Oh, I couldn't. Are you sure? This is so much!"

"Go ahead. Consider it a thank you for helping us out. Though, I'm not sure this really makes up for it…"

"It's plenty! Thank you! I'll dig right in!"

With eyes sparkling so brightly you'd think they were a pair of stars, Elza pressed her hands together and then got to work—by which I meant the task of single-mindedly ferrying what was in front of her into her mouth.

We were at a confectionary shop that apparently had a reputation for the deliciousness of its treats. I say "apparently" because we were here based on the information Rina had given us. It was a secluded, hole-in-the-wall establishment, but all the cakes were exquisitely handmade by the shopkeeper.

Rina wanted treats from here as a souvenir, but she'd written that it would be impossible to preserve them, so we shouldn't go to the trouble. The note had read as extremely reluctant though, so Lorraine had sighed and purchased some anyway. With her storage magic, she could keep perishable food fresh for a week. She'd said it wasn't very practical since it used a lot of mana, but this was a special case. After all, Rina was kind of her pupil too, and probably seemed every bit as adorable to her as Alize. I could sympathize with the feeling.

Elza had never heard of this shop before, and after she'd been given a sample as a taste test, she'd proclaimed to be delighted at the new discovery.

She'd said she wanted to have a proper meal here, so as thanks for her being our guide, we'd seated ourselves in the dining area and offered to treat her. She'd hemmed and hawed over the wide selection of cakes for a while, but after we'd told her she could have as many as she wanted, she'd ordered seven.

Weren't restraint and abbesses meant to go hand in hand? Actually, in the first place, it had to be some kind of sin that an abbess of the Church of the Eastern Sky lost herself to gluttony and sugary temptation, but when I brought the topic up to ask her...

"Lying to oneself is what the Angel hates the most. As long as there is no lie in my heart when I say I wish to eat cake, then I may eat cake."

I got a self-serving excuse as an answer. What was the world coming to, if this was an abbess? From the look on Lorraine's face, she was pondering the question as deeply as I was.

"Whew! I'm full to bursting. I think I could still fit a little more... but I'll save the ones I didn't try as something to look forward to the next time I come here!" Elza patted her stomach and sipped at her remaining tea.

She reminded me of a very pleased-with-itself raccoon dog.

"So long as you're satisfied, I suppose..." Lorraine murmured. "Very well. Shall we call it a day? The sun's beginning to set."

Elza straightened as though she'd recalled something. "Oh, there's still one more thing to do. You said you'd accompany me, remember?"

So she remembered. I thought she'd fall for Lorraine's trap, go with the flow, and leave.

Lorraine smiled. "You're right. Could I ask where we're going, though? You haven't told us."

"You'll find out when we get there—it'll be a surprise. Oh, hold on, I'm going to buy some more cakes as gifts. I'll purchase them myself this time. Thank you again for treating me, by the way."

"Gifts?" I asked.

I wondered who she could be giving them to, but it didn't seem like she was going to answer me. The most likely candidate was whoever we were about to pay a visit to, but she was buying a *lot* of cakes.

"Where do you think we're going?" I whispered to Lorraine.

"Hell if I know. We'll find out when we get there."

She looked drained. Probably because of Elza and how very much not like an abbess she was being. Lorraine wasn't even bothering to speak formally. Then again, we'd decided as we left the abbey earlier that it was more natural to be casual outside anyway. We'd had to mind our manners while we were inside though, or risk coming off as disrespectful. Strangely, Elza was highly respected in the Church.

"Sorry for the wait! Let's go!"

Having finished her purchases, the mountain of cakes in her arms made Elza look like a young mother holding too many children. I could already feel the dirty looks I'd get on the street if I left her to her own devices.

"I'll carry those," I said, taking the cakes from her.

"Oh! I'm really okay...but if you're offering..." Elza smiled, and her absentmindedness vanished in favor of an almost tangible maternal benevolence.

I guessed she wasn't a saint for nothing. The "saint" *I* was more familiar with, on the other hand...

"Hmm? Is there something on my face?" Lorraine tilted her head at me.

"No... Okay, let's get going."

"We're here!"

Our destination was an open space deep into the alleyways of the city. There was an old but tranquil building there, lit up so refreshingly bright that it drove back the gloomy atmosphere of the surrounding alleys.

A number of kids were playing out in front.

"Is this…?"

Before I could finish my question, one of the kids noticed Elza and ran straight for her.

"It's Elza!"

He leaped and clung to her when he reached her, and all the other kids followed suit. In moments, she was practically buried under them. I thought her slender limbs wouldn't be able to support them, but to my surprise, she planted herself firmly on the ground.

Apparently, she was used to this.

"Hey, everyone. Have you been well?"

A chorus of yeses came from the kids.

"I'm glad to hear that. Guess what? I brought you gifts today! Could you all let Sister Mel know that I'm here?"

"Mm-kay! Let's go, everyone!"

A boy who seemed to be the leader of the group led everyone inside the building—an old church, from the look of it—in an energetic scramble.

"This is an orphanage, isn't it?" Lorraine asked.

Elza nodded. "Yes, it is. Lillian and I grew up here."

A short while after watching the kids dash inside, Elza turned to us. "Shall we go in?"

She'd probably decided it would be faster than waiting to be greeted. Since she seemed to be familiar with the cleric who ran the orphanage, at least we wouldn't be barging in as complete strangers.

Elza had been raised here a long time ago, and now that she was abbess, she had another, different kind of connection to the place. She had to be quite comfortable here. That was what I'd gathered from what she'd said, at any rate, along with the general mood.

"Sure," Lorraine and I said, and we went inside.

"Whoa?!"

Upon entering, I abruptly got a faceful of something large and heavy. I'd considered dodging out of the way, but my decision had come too slow since whatever it was didn't seem hostile. It had also been faster than I'd anticipated.

I wondered what it was. I adjusted my head to look, and—

*Pant. Pant. Lick. Lick.*

Hot breath hit my mask along with a wet tongue. Strangely, I didn't feel grossed out. I'd been caught by the tongue of a common *gigantes rana* before—a giant frog, basically—and this ranked way above *that* experience.

Its tongue had been extremely sticky, and I hadn't been able to escape no matter how hard I thrashed about. Eventually, I'd been rescued by a stronger Bronze-class adventurer whom I'd been partied with at the time.

Frog-species monsters were fearsome, despite their comical appearances, and there were theories they'd once been priests in the service of the gods a long time ago. Take them lightly, and they'd make a light meal of you...by licking you to death. What an awful way to go.

Anyway, moving on. Something was licking my face.

"Hey, hey! Pochi! Down, boy!" a gentle voice said.

The large creature backed off from me, and I got my first clear look at it.

"A dog...?"

It was a dog with long white fur. It was huge too—in terms of size, it had Lorraine and me beat. Maalt's guildmaster Wolf came to mind. Yeah, it was about as big as him.

And yet its eyes were friendly and pure. Kind, even. It was adorable. For the record, I was a dog person more than a cat person, so it was no wonder I found it cute. In case you were wondering, Lorraine, like most adventurers, was a cat person. They were less work to take care of, and in some cases, cat-species monsters that were friendly with humans could even make for useful partners.

Meanwhile, dogs were...extreme. There were the obedient breeds that could live happily in a family home, but they had little fighting ability, so if that was what you were after, you'd have to go for the high-ranking monster species.

There was no in-between. It was a bit of a frustrating problem, but if you *could* gain one's loyalty, it would follow you until the day you died, no matter what. There was a sense of security in that.

Cat-species monsters, on the other hand, were fickle, and would abandon you at the first sign of trouble. Either choice left you with a mixed bag of problems and blessings.

A young woman stood by the dog, peering at me and looking concerned.

"Who might you be?" I asked.

Unlike Elza, she was clearly a genuine young person.

"Hey." Elza glared at me, but it only lasted a moment.

Had she read my mind?

"Are you okay?" the young woman asked. "I'm sorry about Pochi. He's usually very docile..."

Hmm. She had a gentle demeanor, a calm air, and a neat and maidenly appearance. Taking everything into account, it would be fair to describe her as a very splendid young lady. She was a little off the mark from my type, but if you asked any group of guys whether they'd want to court her, you'd get an almost one hundred percent thumbs-up rate, Rentt Faina guarantee. The remaining guys would put up a front and say, "Sure, I guess, but only if she confesses first."

We men are stupid like that.

Shaking myself free of silly thoughts, I said, "Are you...sure it's a dog?"

"You know, I'm honestly not quite sure."

"Not sure...?"

"Well, he's just been with us since forever. Since before I came here, even, which was over twenty years ago. He's lived too long to be a normal dog...so he's probably a species of monster."

Ah, so that was what she'd meant. Since I was undead, I'd stopped paying much attention to that kind of thing, but regular animals—creatures with hardly any mana—usually had very fixed life spans. It was generally proportionate to their size within their species. Mammals, for example, tended to live longer the larger they were. This wasn't a hard rule though, and a lot of exceptions existed. Whales lived over a century and dogs around fifteen years, but I'd heard medium-sized dogs lived longer, and that some birds could make it to seventy or eighty, despite their size.

It was a field of study that was ripe for a biologist to harvest. How long one could extend one's life was the eternal question on the minds of living things everywhere.

On the other hand, when it came to monsters... Well, I doubted I had anything like a "natural life span." I was undead. Still, even if I wasn't, monsters tended to live longer than animals on the whole.

It was said that mana prolonged a creature's life, but the reality was that it was uncertain.

Fanatical scholars had bred animals in mana-dense environments, injected their blood with mana-dense liquids, and conducted all kinds of mad experiments. Lorraine had done some of that herself. However, despite many such trials being carried out through history, the current prevailing answer was still "results undetermined."

In the end, nothing was known about the definitions separating people, animals, and monsters.

If you told that to a scholar, they'd attempt to prove you wrong by pointing out differences here, commonalities there, that kind of thing. But though their faces would grow red and their voices would become scathing as they pointed to obvious scientific research and evidence, their *theories* wouldn't hold up for a decade before being proven wrong.

This process had been repeated dozens, hundreds of times over history. So what were monsters, really? Nobody knew. But something told me that this huge "dog" which had lived healthily for over twenty years was one.

"Woof, woof!"

[Hello!]

So you could understand my shock when it began talking to me.

Did the dog just talk? Technically speaking, I supposed it was actually a dog-species monster. But even then, it was strange that it talked. Civilization wasn't unheard of among monsters; goblin species established settlements and occasionally even learned human speech.

It stood to reason that humanoid monsters also had humanoid organs, so if they made the effort to talk, they probably could. Aside from myself, Isaac and Laura would also fit in that category. Nevertheless, matters were different when it came to animalistic monsters. Only the higher-ranked ones were capable of speech.

It was said that, in such cases, they either used their own vocal cords or spoke through an ability called telepathy.

The one in front of me—Pochi, was it?—had clearly barked like a dog vocally, but...I wondered which method he'd used.

Surprised, I said, "Did anyone else just...?"

"Hmm? Is something the matter?" the young woman who'd stopped Pochi earlier asked.

"Well, yeah, I mean... Hmm?"

From her reaction, she didn't seem to have noticed the dog talking. Had it just been me?

"Rentt," Lorraine said. "*For the time being*, why don't we introduce ourselves first?"

So it hadn't just been my imagination.

There was a lot of power in the phrase "for the time being." It would have sounded normal to everyone else, but I'd picked up on the hidden implication. That we could communicate like this just went to show how long Lorraine and I had known each other. She'd heard the dog speak too.

"You're right," I said. "Where are my manners? I'm Rentt, and this is Lorraine. We make a living as adventurers."

I left "And you are?" unsaid, but the young woman with a firm grasp on the dog recognized the cue.

"I'm Mel Patiche, the director of Vistelya's Third Orphanage, which is where we are now. This is Pochi. And these are…"

She looked at the kids, and they began to introduce themselves, one by one.

There were more than a dozen of them, but I managed to remember their names…or at least, I thought I did. It was an invaluable skill for an adventurer. If you couldn't get a handle on it, you'd be in trouble whenever you joined up with a random party for a job.

It went without saying that Lorraine had learned the kids' names by heart within moments. She was nothing like me, who struggled to memorize mnemonics. Sometimes, I wished she'd share some of her brains with me.

"And I'm Elza Olgado," Elza said, concluding the introductions. "Though, you already knew that. Now, come on everyone, I brought gifts. There's enough for everybody."

She pointed the kids toward the stacks of cakes, which had at some point transferred from my arms to Lorraine's. They immediately surrounded her and began taking them from her hands as though they were bandits robbing her of all her worldly possessions.

"Even bandits would show more consideration," Lorraine muttered after they were done. Her hair was tousled and her breathing was ragged.

She was joking, of course. Real bandits would be in for a nasty surprise if they attacked her. Nevertheless, she'd been mobbed so enthusiastically that the comparison had been appropriate.

The kids that had swept over Lorraine like a storm disappeared elsewhere with their spoils.

"I think they're headed for the kitchen," Elza explained. "They'll bring some back out for us, with tea too."

That they went to prepare the food showed that they were fairly used to this. I wondered if Elza always dropped by with gifts.

"What's the occasion today, Sister Elza?" Mel asked. "You don't have any companions with you."

I figured she wasn't including Lorraine and me in that because we'd introduced ourselves as adventurers.

Elza was an abbess. Her companions would obviously be clerics and attendants from the Church of the Eastern Sky. Most adventurers were rough around the edges, so they'd never make the cut to become an attendant of a member of the nobility or clergy. Bodyguards, sure, but then the client would still need their attendants.

That was especially true for a high-ranking member of the clergy like Elza. Nonetheless, she was currently unaccompanied. No wonder Mel found this strange.

"If I'd brought them, they would've never stopped nagging me about the time," Elza said. Then she grinned. "Just kidding, of course. I just wanted to bring these two here today. They're acquaintances of Lillian from Maalt."

"What? Really?!" Mel turned to us. "How is Sister Lillian? I write to her, but she never replies."

Elza had said something similar.

Lillian hadn't replied to Elza because she'd been dispatched to the frontier due to a power struggle in Vistelya's Church of the Eastern Sky. If she'd written back, it could have meant trouble for Elza. The same likely applied to Mel too.

"That's not a concern anymore," Elza said. "Lillian has regained her strength. She even sent me a letter."

Elza held out the letter we'd brought from Maalt to Mel, whose eyes widened before she reached out to touch it.

"It feels familiar…" Mel murmured.

"Lillian's divinity is in it," Elza explained. "Most of it faded after I opened it, but there's still a little left."

"Really? Thank goodness she's well. Does this mean she'll be returning eventually?"

"I'm…not sure. But should she choose to, nobody would be able to object anymore. And even if she doesn't want to return, she'd be free to come and go for visits. I'm sure you'll see her again."

"Oh, I can't wait!" Mel hugged the letter to herself.

She seemed to adore Lillian, and I found myself curious. I wondered what their story was.

"Mel came to this orphanage as a child just before Lillian left for the church," Elza explained. "After joining the clergy, both Lillian and I still made regular visits here to help out. Mel's something of a sister to us, or maybe a daughter."

So Lillian, Elza, and Mel were essentially sisters. In which case, they must have felt terribly sad about not being able to keep in contact.

Since Lillian's orphanage was under the authority of the Church of the Eastern Sky and Elza held quite a high position, the latter could check whether the former was still alive any time she wanted. But that was nothing compared to seeing that your sister was okay with your own two eyes.

Elza wouldn't be able to go to a remote area like Maalt, and Mel wouldn't be able to leave her duties at the orphanage. Unlike the Church of Lobelia, the Church of the Eastern Sky didn't have deep pockets. The number of orphanage employees they could maintain was limited. And while Eastern Sky clerics were beloved in Yaaran and the people assisted them in all manner of ways, there was some orphanage work that outsiders couldn't handle.

Making the trip to see Lillian would mean leaving the orphanage unattended for weeks. Maalt wasn't exactly close to Vistelya. Lorraine and I could make the trip in an instant via teleportation circles, and part of me really wanted to help the sisters, but there was too much risk of the secret getting out. Elza herself seemed trustworthy, but she was a high-ranking member of the Church of the Eastern Sky. I couldn't discount the possibility that she'd be willing to put the church's benefit first if the time ever came.

"It's a shame Lillian didn't write you a letter too, if you're that close," I said. "Not that I don't appreciate your circumstances. And Lillian herself was pretty sick until recently, anyway."

Mel's expression grew concerned. "What? I-Is Sister Lillian okay?"

"We've told Elza already, but she had Accumulative Miasma Disease. Not anymore, though. She's okay now."

"Isn't that quite difficult to cure? If I remember right, you need…"

"Dragon Blood Blossoms, yeah. I picked some for her, and a great herbalist turned it into medicine for her. She's in the clear now, up and about and running the orphanage."

"Really?! Then Sister Lillian's in your debt, which means I am too! Thank you, Rentt!"

"No, well…"

It really wasn't that big a deal. The request had been a good experience for me, and it was how I'd met Isaac, and then Laura.

Maybe I'd have come across them at a later time regardless, but who knows what kind of trouble I'd have run into if I hadn't met them early on? It wasn't an exaggeration to say that I was who I was today because I'd taken Alize's request.

I turned to Elza. "That aside, did you bring us here so we could talk about Lillian?"

"Yes. I was wondering if you'd be willing to tell us about her life in Maalt. I could have asked you earlier, but I wanted Mel to be here too." Elza smiled. "Also, I wanted you to help carry the shopping."

I was pretty sure that last part had been a joke. Maybe her true thoughts had leaked in a little though. It definitely would have been tough for her to carry all those cakes alone. Less because of the weight, and more because of the bulk.

"Sure, I can tell you about Lillian," I said. "Lorraine can too."

She'd taken Alize as her apprentice too, so Lorraine had her own relationship with Lillian. She'd occasionally donate surplus magic items and potions, stuff like that. There was a good chance she saw Lillian more than I did.

"I'd be happy to," Lorraine said.

We spent a while chatting happily about Lillian. It wasn't just us—Elza and Mel joined in with stories about her time as a child at this orphanage, as well as her time in the church. However, the topic of why Lillian had been driven out of the capital was never broached. I supposed it was an internal church matter.

According to Elza and Mel, Lillian had been quite active as a girl, to the point she'd basically made them her lackeys. At the same time, she'd been a caring older sister that everybody in the orphanage had loved.

I'd sensed that at Maalt's orphanage too. When you were inside, it felt like you couldn't disobey her. The kids never acted out against her either. These days, she was always mild-mannered and friendly, and it seemed as though her rascal side was gone, but maybe the kids had sensed it still lurking inside her.

After a pleasant time spent laughing and chatting…

"I think we'll have to call it a day. Oh, and I completely forgot. Here."

Elza produced a letter from her breast pocket and held it out to me. It was firmly sealed and gave off a faint aura of divinity. It was no surprise, but Elza had sealed her letter just as Lillian had.

That meant they'd find out if I opened it to take a look. Not that I would, so they really didn't need to go to the bother.

*Sniff. Sniff.*

Pochi, who had been lying down behind Mel doing his best couch impression, had gotten up and was sniffing the letter. I watched him, wondering what had caught his attention, but evidently a few sniffs had been enough to satisfy him.

"Woof, woof."

[Good.]

I knew I hadn't just been imagining things.

"You don't have to worry yourself so much, Pochi," Elza said. "My seals aren't so easy to break."

"Woof?"

[You think?]

"I do."

Was it just me, or were they having a conversation? Some of my doubt must have shown on my face, because Elza suddenly spoke to me next.

"I knew it. You can hear him, can't you, Rentt?"

"H-Hear wh-wh-what?"

I trembled as I spoke, because I'd just seen something extremely shocking. That was why I was stammering too. Yep, I was definitely shocked at—

"You can drop the act," Elza said calmly. "I'm talking about Pochi's words. You understand him, right?"

I sighed. "I guess. I thought it was my imagination, but apparently not. How can a dog talk...?"

I'd tried to play dumb when she'd first asked me, but one look at her gaze had told me it wasn't going to work. Despite seeming irresponsible, she really was a high-ranking clergy member when it counted. I knew a lost battle when I saw one.

As for my ridiculous act, I'd thought a little goofiness would be fine since things didn't seem like they were going to get heavy, and I'd also wanted to draw attention away from Lorraine, since Elza seemed to have noticed only me.

In fact, Lorraine was utterly composed. Her mildly curious expression screamed, "Oh, whatever is going on? I'm not quite sure." What an actress.

"Um, is something wrong? What do you mean 'Pochi's words'?"

As for Sister Mel, she looked genuinely clueless.

I'd thought she could hear Pochi too, but maybe I'd been wrong. In which case, what separated those who could and those who couldn't?

Elza turned to Mel. "I've been telling you since forever, haven't I? Pochi can talk. Only Lillian and I could ever hear him though."

"What?! That was real? I thought you two were just teasing me..."

Oh, that made sense. It wasn't that Mel hadn't known, but that she hadn't believed them. Family messed with each other wherever you went. Getting tricked into believing a tall tale by a parent, sibling, or another relative only for them to come to you later and say "Got you!" was exactly what Mel had thought was happening here.

"That dog can talk!" was the textbook example of a lie like that. Eventually, Mel would've started rolling her eyes and brushing it off, saying, "The usual, huh? Sure, sure." It was a ritual as old as time.

"Sure, I teased you about other things, but never about Pochi. He really can talk." Elza leaned her ear toward Pochi. "Hmm, what was that?"

"Woof, woof, woof woof, bark. Bark bark, bark bark, woof woof woof. Woof."

[Get this. Mel snuck some sweets for herself the other day, and then later on she got worried about whether she'd put on weight. Isn't that hilarious?]

I felt guilty that I could hear all of this. Also, wow, this dog had a bit of a twisted personality, didn't he?

"Mel," Elza said, "you should stop sneaking sweets for yourself. Also, you haven't gained weight. You're just...a little rounder."

Mel looked aghast. "H-How do you know that?! I made sure nobody saw me! Only— Wait, Pochi?! It was you?! You can really...?!"

I took the yelling to mean that she finally believed what Elza had been trying to tell her for years.

Mel grabbed Pochi's face. "Was it you who told them about the other thing too?! Remember?! I'd never told anybody about it, but somehow Elza and Lillian knew anyway!"

She was interrogating Pochi ruthlessly. You'd never think she was the director of the orphanage with the way she was acting. The initial gentle and maidenly demeanor she'd had was completely gone. Or maybe that was just a testament to how frantic she felt. It was hard to tell.

Ignoring the ongoing dispute between dog and orphanage director, Elza turned to Lorraine and me. "There you have it. Pochi can talk, but only some people can hear him. From this orphanage, it was only ever Lillian and I. Do you know why?"

I honestly didn't have an answer for her. There were a number of points in common between Elza and me, but that got messier when you added Lorraine into the mix.

Actually, I *did* have one idea that seemed likely. However, it would mean spilling my own secrets, so I decided to give a wrong answer on purpose.

"Was it when you two became clerics of the church?"

"That's...close, but not quite it. I don't think dragging this out would do any good, so I'll just tell you. It's because—"

"Hey! Why am I the only one who can't hear you?! Pochi! I've been with you way longer than Sister Elza and Sister Lillian! Who do you think feeds you, hmm?! And I've always been the one to give you baths since I was little! So why?!" Mel was getting more and more heated, clinging to Pochi as she aired out all her grievances.

Pochi looked extremely fed up. He glanced at me, then made eye contact with Eliza.

Eliza sighed, thought for a moment, and said, "I suppose there's nothing for it. This was going to happen one day anyway. I've climbed quite high in the church, and Lillian's back too. We should be able to deal with the consequences."

She turned to Pochi and nodded.

Just as I was beginning to wonder what was happening, Pochi suddenly began to glow faintly. The light was tranquil, pure... and familiar.

When Lorraine saw it, she murmured, "Rentt. That's divinity."

I realized she was right. It was never very strong when I used it myself, and I'd taken to hiding even that ever since I'd learned how to, so these days mine was invisible. The last time I'd seen divinity on this scale was that saint who'd come to Maalt and showed off her healing magic as a form of advertisement.

I'd seen Nive's divinity too, but hers didn't really shine. Probably because she was well practiced with it.

But was this dog doing what I thought it was doing? After a short time, the light transferred to Mel and was absorbed into her.

"Woof?"

[How is it?]

Mel opened her eyes. "I-I can hear him! I can hear Pochi!" Then she hugged him.

Elza watched them as she said, "There you go. Pochi's...what people would call a divine, or sacred, beast, which makes him akin to divine spirits. Only those who have received the blessing of divinity can hear him. That includes you, doesn't it, Rentt?"

## Side Story:   The Disquieting Woman

A few years ago, when I was still making a living as a human adventurer of Yaaran...

"She wants you to take her to Rook Cape?" I asked. I was at Lorraine's place having dinner. "Remind me why she wants to go there again?"

"She wants to see the view from there, apparently," Lorraine replied. "Well, strange jobs are a copper a dozen. Adventurers such as ourselves can't be too picky about the details, though we'll be careful to look out for anything suspicious, of course."

We were talking about a job Lorraine had accepted. A woman by the name of Hilde had requested an escort to a remote area called Rook Cape.

The strange thing about the job was that nobody ever went there. No towns or villages existed in the area, and neither did any dungeons. There was no particular specialty that could be found there either...unless you counted the scenery, which, granted, *was* beautiful.

There was also one more thing about Rook Cape...

"Funny you should mention caution..." I murmured. "Do you think she'll be okay?"

"You're worried about it happening too, are you? It'd be nice to not have to consider it and let her be, but I'd rather not accidentally see something unpleasant."

"So you are getting that feeling, huh?"

We were talking about whether this Hilde woman was planning on throwing herself off the cape.

Geographically, Rook Cape was an outcropping that jutted out high above a large lake—Lake Quia.

Because of this, it was known as a common suicide spot. It wasn't too far from the town of Maalt—a two-day journey on foot, if you pushed yourself, but this was just far enough to create a sense of distance. For those who'd made up their minds, it was a place where nobody could get in the way.

From that point of view, it would seem that there was no need to worry, though, since the client had requested an escort.

I brought that up to Lorraine. "Still, she wouldn't go out of her way to hire an escort if she was going to do it, right?"

"That'd be true if she were a man, maybe. There's always the chance that a lone woman would get snatched by bandits during the journey. Maybe she's just making absolutely sure. Just because she might want to die doesn't mean she'd want to be taken by bandits."

"Ah, right..."

In my head, I'd had the preconceived notion that nothing else really mattered if you were going to die anyway, but Lorraine was right that there were absolutely some things you'd rather avoid.

"Okay, I get the picture now," I said. "Just stay on your toes. If you can convince her not to..."

"I can promise I'm ready to stop her and hear her story, at least. I'm not so busy I can't make the time for that."

"Good to hear."

"Oh, Rentt!"

Early the next day, when I went to the guild, an employee called out to me.

"Something wrong?" I asked.

"You haven't taken a job yet, have you?"

"No, I was just about to."

"Then could I ask you to fill a vacancy on another job? It was short notice."

I wasn't unfamiliar with the situation. While many adventurers in Maalt were the diligent type, the profession inherently attracted rowdy people. In other words, sometimes you'd get adventurers who'd cancel on a job without any prior warning. The cleanup for that would then fall to the guild and its employees to handle.

I looked at the employee's face. I felt a little bad for them.

"Sure," I said. "I don't mind. But could you tell me about the job first?"

"Oh! Thank you! Okay, so…"

The guild employee explained the details of the job, and I found myself surprised. It matched the details of the job Lorraine and I had talked about just yesterday. The vacancy was an adventurer who had been intended to be the wagon driver but could no longer be found.

If that was all the job was, then I figured I'd be fine.

"Got it," I said. "I'll take it. Where should I go?"

"You're meeting at the wagon staging area. You should hurry. It's almost time."

"Will do. I'll head there now!"

As I ran off, I heard the guild employee's voice call out behind me.

"Thank you so much!"

"So you're the replacement?" Lorraine asked when I reached the wagon staging area. "Hilde, are you okay with him?"

Hilde was a young woman. She didn't look like she was suicidal, but then again, I didn't know a thing about women's emotions. They were simply unfathomable.

"Yes, I don't mind. It doesn't seem as though we have another option, anyway..."

"We could always postpone it to another day."

"I'm afraid not. I'd like to be there by this evening."

"In that case, this is our only option. It should be fine though. This man—Rentt's reliable when it comes to his work."

"Is he an acquaintance of yours?"

"It's more like we can't get rid of each other..."

"Then I have even less to be concerned about. It's a pleasure to meet you, Rentt."

Hilde smiled and held her hand out to me, so I shook it.

"R-Right. Good to meet you too."

The wagon was a rental that Hilde had hired. She'd already paid the fee, so all that would be left to do was drop it off upon our return to Maalt.

I was a little wary about how well she seemed to be tying up loose ends, but the more we spoke to her, the more I realized that I had nothing to worry about. She wasn't suicidal at all.

Then, despite Lorraine and I having done our best to hide our concern, Hilde asked, "Um, is something bothering you?"

Lorraine, perhaps thinking that we might as well come clean given how far we'd come already, explained, her tone slightly nervous.

After a few moments of silence, Hilde burst into laughter.

"Aha ha ha! I get it now! Ha ha ha! Now that you've pointed it out, I can understand why you'd think that. A lone woman traveling to Rook Cape... I suppose it does seem like that kind of place. Still, rest assured. I don't intend to do any such thing."

"I-Is that so? That's good to hear..." Lorraine said. "But now I must admit I'm even more curious as to what your goal is."

Rook Cape had nothing but a good view. It wasn't a place worth making the effort to go to, yet that was what she was doing.

"Normally, that's how it would seem, yes," Hilde said. "But, hmm. You know, I was originally going to enjoy it alone, but why don't you two join me? Are you good at hiding yourselves?"

Though we were unsure why she was asking, Lorraine and I nodded.

Rook Cape, at night. Under the moonlight, we hid ourselves as we watched the lake.

"Really?" Lorraine asked. "In a place like this?"

"Yes," Hilde replied. "Every year on this day, without fail. The story's been passed down in my family since my great-grandmother's generation. I come every year."

"I haven't seen your job postings," I pointed out.

"I usually ask an adventurer party I know, but not long ago, they went to the capital, so..."

"Ah, right... Oh, look! Seriously...?"

In the midst of our conversation, a peculiar presence began to rise from the lake. It took the form of a mighty monster—one that everybody knew the name of.

"A dragon," Lorraine breathed. "An...ice dragon, if I'm right. Who could've known one lived here of all places?"

It was an honest-to-goodness ice dragon. But the wonders didn't end there.

"It sounds like it's singing..." I said.

Its cry echoed throughout the surroundings like a song. It was beautiful; I never would've guessed it to be a dragon's cry if I hadn't known.

"I've heard before that certain species of dragon cry like that when courting a mate," Lorraine said. "But I had no idea when or where they did it..."

"Look, it's coming!" Hilde exclaimed.

Another dragon descended from the skies. This one was an ice dragon too, but it had wings, making it look like a different species entirely.

"Those wings..." Lorraine murmured, her tone becoming analytical. "They're made of ice. So they use those to fly, and use the songs to guide them to their mates? That's a fascinating element of their ecology. From the look of it, I think the one in the lake is the female."

Then, the pair of ice dragons sank deep beneath the water.

"Grandmother said they probably couple down there," Hilde said.

Lorraine nodded. "They likely do. Otherwise, with their massive bodies, they'd tear up the ground and make a ruckus that would attract attention. In the lake...they could even build barriers."

"It'd be rude to peek, of course. Now then, let's head back."

"That's it?" I asked.

"Yes. I only came here to hear the song. I don't want to interrupt the newlyweds."

"Mmm," Lorraine hummed. "You're right. I suppose we should go. You're driver again, Rentt."

"Yeah...I know."

After we returned to Maalt, we parted ways with Hilde. She told us that she'd like to commission us again next year, if we were still around, and Lorraine agreed.

We were back in Lorraine's home, and she had a satisfied expression on her face.

"That was an excellent job," she said.

I nodded and asked, "Because you learned something you didn't know about monster ecology?"

"Mmm. Maalt's great for occasional discoveries like that. There are so many novel experiences on the frontier. Perhaps I'll start taking jobs more actively starting tomorrow..."

"I'm all for you doing that, but I suspect the good ones are rarer than you expect... That aside, I was doing some thinking, and I realized something kind of scary."

"What?"

"That lake's a suicide spot, right? And a dragon lives there."

"Ah. So after the suicide happens... Perhaps we shouldn't think about this too hard."

"Yeah. Let's just forget it."

"Couldn't agree more."

# Afterword

Thank you very much for purchasing *The Unwanted Undead Adventurer: Volume 11*!

Hello, I'm Yu Okano. Volume 10 of the manga is also out on sale now, so if you feel so inclined, I'd be overjoyed if you picked up a copy!

I'm over the moon that the manga and novel have surpassed the ten-volume mark!

The anime adaptation has been decided as well, and it's been nothing but good things for me lately, so sometimes I get scared that something bad's going to come along soon. I can't help but worry about everything… I have a terribly nervous temperament…

Now that I think about it, I've been like this ever since I was a young child. For example, I'd always worry about whether I forgot something on school trips or excursions. I also worried about things like whether I'd forgotten my textbooks for tomorrow or my swimsuit.

However, back then, my worry stemmed from not wanting the teacher to yell at me. I don't think it was worry for worry's sake. In fact, despite my concerns, I still forgot things a lot…but I guess that's what you'd call a habit. Perhaps because I've lived my life thinking, "I don't want to forget anything," over and over, I've become a person who dreads forgetting things. I even get awfully worried about whether I locked the front door to my house five minutes ago… despite the fact that I most certainly did.

Another similar characteristic of mine is that I'm a germophobe. I didn't have this problem as a child, but now that I'm an adult, I don't want to enter a house unless I've thoroughly scrubbed my hands with soap. The idea of coming in from outside and lying on my bed with my outdoor clothes on is unthinkable to me! That's more or less the typical type of germophobe I became.

If I had to come up with a reason, it probably began with my living on my own. When you're living with your family, it's hard to truly become a germophobe because they're always touching stuff and leaving it around anyway. But when you live alone, everything in your house is yours and you're free to do what you want, so if something is even a millimeter out of place, it starts bothering you...

I don't know if this is a good or bad thing, but considering recent world events, perhaps it's a good habit to develop...

What was I talking about again? Oh, right, habits and obsession. If you're wondering why I'm telling you about this, I'd say it's because my writing is similar. Some of you know that I'm a web novel writer and that I post my writing online regularly.

When I first started, I only wrote occasionally, but before I realized, it had become a habit. Just like my habit of worrying whether I'd forgotten anything. Then, as I wrote my stories, my obsession over them grew, perhaps because I could direct everything to be exactly how I wanted. I wouldn't be satisfied until I'd written all the fine details just right. It's almost like being a germaphobe. But lately, I've been thinking that too much of either is a bad thing.

Perhaps, since overdoing things causes us to lose our limits, we have to determine the right time and place to stop for ourselves.

In that sense, working on books like this serves as good stopping points for me.

Deadlines, manuscript tweaking, handing it to the proofreader, illustrations… Not everything goes precisely how I want it to, but I feel like that's what actually leads to harmony.

Anyway, that was how *The Unwanted Undead Adventurer: Volume 11* was completed. I hope you enjoyed it, and I'll see you in the next volume.

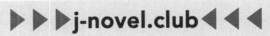

# J-Novel Club Lineup

## Latest Ebook Releases Series List